To Rina —
my best friend
always.
Love Carol

2012

In loving memory
of my mother,
Lillian Edwards,
who taught me
how to knit.

Published in 2011 by Stewart, Tabori & Chang
An imprint of ABRAMS

Text and illustrations copyright ©
Michelle Edwards

Photographs copyright © 2011 Jen Gotch

Versions of "Only Wool" and "Lillian
Edwards" have appeared in Lion Brand Yarn'
e-newsletter.

Library of Congress Cataloging
in Publication Division

Edwards, Michelle.
A knitter's home companion / Michelle
Edwards; photographs by Jen Gotch.
    p. cm.
 ISBN 978-1-58479-916-0 (alk. paper)
1. Knitting--Patterns. 2. Knitting--
Miscellanea. I. Title.
TT820.E47 2011
746.43'2--dc22
2010020942

Editor: Melanie Falick
Technical Editor: Sue McCain
Designer: onethread
Production Manager: Tina Cameron

The text of this book was composed in
Gotham and Archer.

Printed and bound in the U.S.A.

10 9 8 7 6 5 4 3 2

Stewart, Tabori & Chang books are available at special discounts when purchased in
quantity for premiums and promotions
as well as fundraising or educational
use. Special editions can also be created
to specification. For details, contact
specialsales@abramsbooks.com or
the address below.

ABRAMS
THE ART OF BOOKS SINCE 1949

115 West 18th Street
New York, NY 10011
www.abramsbooks.com

A KNITTER'S HOME COMPANION

A HEARTWARMING COLLECTION OF STORIES, PATTERNS, AND RECIPES

MICHELLE EDWARDS

PHOTOGRAPHS
BY JEN GOTCH

STC Craft | A Melanie Falick Book

Stewart, Tabori & Chang
New York

CONTENTS

PROJECTS

RECIPES

WELCOME

Eventually, I gave up. My husband, Rody, loves languages and learning new things. He's interested in a wide range of topics. But as hard as I have tried, knitting has not become one of them.

My daughters, Meera, Flory, and Lelia, are a little better. When a new knitting magazine arrives in the mail, I can usually corral one of them into looking through it with me, asking them to weigh in on what they like most or least. Lately they are a bit more willing to indulge me, interested in snagging a pair of hand-knitted socks or wristers—occasionally, a sweater. None of them show any sustained inclination to pick up the needles and make something for themselves, or—sigh—me. And although I love them dearly, they have not grown into knitting buddies.

These days if I need to blab about a great new yarn or find a sympathetic ear for complaints about a sweater that refuses to be finished, I talk to other knitters. I e-mail one. I head down for a cup of tea at the Home Ec Workshop, which knitters in my town are known to frequent. If it's a Saturday and I'm not needed on the home front, I'll join the Fae Ridge Knitters on Janette Ryan-Busch's organic farm out on Rapid Creek Road. Or I start an essay for my monthly gig with the Lion Brand Yarn Company e-newsletter.

Knitting is like belonging to a tribe complete with initiation rituals, customs, rites of passage, and language. After knitting awhile, you acquire strong opinions about thumbs, gussets, and heels. And when you have been knitting for a long time, like I have, knitting shapes your worldview. Reading a picture book about a chair a family buys for the mother, I think about the chair I knit in. The main character in a movie appears in a handmade hat, and I stray from the plot, lost in the hat's cables. Given an afghan made by an aunt I never really knew, I translate its colors, size, and pattern and discover a kindred spirit. Story ideas percolate when I knit socks for a friend, unfold the baby blanket I made my firstborn, or untangle a skein of yarn.

Knitting is not just a metaphor. Knitting is a life. And because my knitting flows into what I draw and write, what I cook, and what I read, this illustrated gathering of my stories is connected to recipes, patterns, and books. Let it keep you company when you need another knitter's voice beside you. Stick it in your knitting bag, and pull it out when you are waiting in a doctor's office. Use it to help you through a lonely moment—when you're away from your knitting group, when your favorite yarn store is closed, or when it's too late to call your best buddy in New York City—or China.

Welcome to *A Knitter's Home Companion*. Thanks for stopping by.

CHAPTER 1

Motherhood

MEERA'S BLANKET

RODY AND I WERE MARRIED ON A COLD NOVEMBER EVENING— too cold to wear just my wedding dress and the shawl I had made, but that's all I wore anyway. The new shawl was my stretch to meet the bridal tradition of something old, something new, something borrowed, something blue. The wool was pale rose, not blue, but the pattern was borrowed from a shawl belonging to my friend and mentor, Isabel Nirenberg. And the something old was the tradition of the handmade passed on to me from my mother, who taught me to knit. She had died less than a year before, a decade after my father's death. Rody's parents were also deceased. We were on our own.

We planned for our wedding to take place where we lived together, in Iowa City, a Big Ten university town. We made double sure that our chosen date wasn't during a home football game weekend. We reserved a block of hotel rooms for our out-of-town guests, and the Hillel House, the Jewish student center where I worked, for the wedding. We hired a band and a caterer for the reception. Mr. Rubinstein, the cantor who had prepared Rody and his brother, Myron, for their bar mitzvahs, flew in to help with the ceremony.

We exchanged our vows in front of a gathering of family and neighbors, old friends and new ones. Later, while the band played, the same group cheered and clapped as the crew of Iranian students I had invited seated us in chairs and lifted us up for a traditional marriage dance. My handmade shawl, tossed aside during the night's warmth and excitement, felt perfect back on my shoulders as Rody and I, husband and wife, stepped out into the cold again.

Our honeymoon was to be a few weeks later. We had found a great package deal to Denmark between Christmas and New Year's. The day we were to leave, the Maharishi University in Fairfield, Iowa, about an hour and a half south of our house, orchestrated a worldwide meditation to generate world peace. Sadly, instead of global harmony, Iowa was hit by a temperature freeze so spectacular that our plane was unable to fuel up. As we waited to check our luggage, all flights out were canceled. It was neither practical, nor possible, to catch up with our connection in Chicago by car.

At a restaurant near the airport, while sipping hot chocolate, we planned our honeymoon once again. Maybe a new destination would change our luck. Rody had lived and studied in Portugal and spoke the language. His stories of the country, the food, and the people won me over. We decided on Portugal in April, when travel would be safe from the vagaries of winter weather on the prairie and the interference of any international peace efforts.

It was a wonderful choice. Our plane left on time, and we arrived in Lisbon on a warm spring day. We drank coffee in charming cafés and walked cobblestone streets that looked like they came from a fairy tale. In the northern city of Oporto, we sipped port, and I found a small yarn store. Inside, glowing from their cubbies and baskets were the lightest, softest bundles of vibrant greens, blues, and pinks. Not knowing or even thinking about what I might make with it, I bought a palette of the fine-weight wool.

I didn't really have a stash back then. I had been a poor graduate student when Rody and I had met, and I bought yarn judiciously. But I wasn't a poor student anymore. I had earned my master of fine arts degree in printmaking, and my part-time job at Hillel paid what felt like a huge salary to me. Rody, as he has always been fond of saying, was also "gainfully employed." In a very modest way, I was a woman of means. I could buy yarn when I felt like it.

Other changes, ones I could not control, had hurled me into adulthood. My mother's death was still a very deep hurting hole. The house where I spent most of my growing-up years now belonged to another family. The part of my life as someone's daughter was over, and a new part, as someone's wife and partner, was just taking root. My Portuguese honeymoon, I decided, and my colorful new stash of yarn, marked this new chapter. When we returned home, I stored it in our front-hall closet, leaving the bag open so I could eye the yarn when I shrugged on a coat or reached for an umbrella. Someday, I would make something special with it.

Four years later, I was pregnant. That's when I took out my bag of yarn from Portugal. This was what I had been saving it for—to make something for a baby. Not a sweater she would outgrow in a month or two, or booties she would kick off and lose, but something more lasting, like a blanket that she might sleep with and treasure her whole life.

One at a time, I opened each skein, slipping the glory of a blue, a green, and two pinks over the back of our dining-room chairs. Rody kept me company. Hand-rolling about a million yards of the fine Portuguese wool into balls, with an occasional break to drink the tea he brewed us, was a task that took me almost an entire evening. But I was an expert; I used to do this all the time for my mother. With an assembly of beautiful yarn on my dining-room table and the skills my mother had passed on to me, I moved toward being a mother myself, and carrying a tradition of the handmade to the next generation.

I picked a very simple pattern, one my mother and I had once used to make an afghan together. The new blanket was a joyous ride of color, and I was about half done when, six weeks before my due date, Rody was offered a better job. On New Year's Day, we moved to St. Paul, Minnesota. Friends brought by baby things early, so we could take them with us: toys, car seats, a crib, baby clothes, and an assortment of blankets, all gently used by their children and now lovingly passed on to ours.

We stayed at a hotel in downtown St. Paul until our house was ready. By midafternoon each day, the Minnesota winter sky was already darkening. In our room, watching the city lights turn on one by one, I would work on the blanket. It was finished before we settled into our house. We were ready for this baby.

Meera Lil was born on February 28, 1987, named for Rody's father, Milton, and my mother, Lillian. Two days after her birth, we wrapped our Meera in the blanket I had made her and left the hospital as a family. In the round-the-clock nursing that followed, I used the blanket to cover her, its colors a vivid contrast against the tiny puff of her dark hair.

Meera's blanket is a sturdy one. Honestly, a tad stiff. A larger gauge would have given it a much better drape. As she grew bigger, I would often tuck her in with the much softer machine-made blankets my Iowa City pals had given us. And at some point, the white acrylic one with the silky trim became the one Meera always wanted. Rubbing the silky strip helped her fall asleep. Early on, it earned from her the coveted name "Blankie." Over the years, I have repaired Meera's Blankie, patching holes and replacing the silk edging. The blanket itself is now in shreds; clinging to it is a few less-than-pristine remains of its once smooth and shiny borders. Still, nothing could ever convince Meera to give up her Blankie. Even now, she guards the traces of it.

I keep watch over the blanket I created for her all those years ago. Meera's blanket, like the ones I later made for her younger sisters, Flory and Lelia, wasn't just a baby blanket, and it wasn't just for her. All three of them were for me, too. They were my expressions of hope for these new lives after the loss of my parents, my family anchors. These blankets never won a place in my children's hearts; they never were their "blankies," but they have served me well as artifacts of who I was in my early days of motherhood. Meera's blanket is folded and stored in the cedar hope chest that once belonged to Rody's mother. Lelia's and Flory's are there, too. Taken out again and again, to help me remember, they always do their job. And that seems like more than enough for a blanket to be able to do.

ZIGZAG BABY BLANKET

MAKING A BABY BLANKET IS AS MUCH A GIFT FOR THE knitter as it is for the baby. Unlike the original blanket for Meera (my oldest daughter, now a college graduate), this one is worked at a large gauge so it can be finished easily before the baby arrives. If you are new to color knitting, follow the pattern chart carefully; within a few rows, you'll likely have it memorized.

. . . .

FINISHED MEASUREMENTS
29" wide x 32" long, lightly blocked

YARN
Lion Brand Homespun (98% acrylic / 2% polyester; 185 yards / 170 grams): 2 skeins #399 Apple Green (MC)

Lion Brand Yarn Jiffy (100% acrylic; 135 yards / 85 grams): 2 skeins #099 Fisherman (A)

NEEDLES
One 29" (70 cm) long or longer circular (circ) needle size US 10½ (6.5 mm)
Change needle size if necessary to obtain correct gauge.

NOTIONS
Stitch markers (optional)

GAUGE
14 sts and 16 rows = 4" (10 cm) in Two-Color Zigzag, lightly blocked

☐ Knit on RS, purl on WS.

▣ Knit on WS.

▨ MC

☐ A

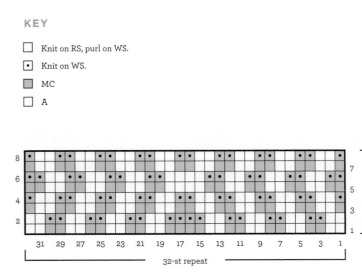

STITCH PATTERN

Two-Color Zigzag (see Chart)

(multiple of 32 sts; 8-row repeat)

Row 1 (RS): [K2 A, k2 MC] 3 times, k2 A, k4 MC, [k2 A, k2 MC] 3 times, k2 A.

Row 2: [P2 A, k2 MC] 3 times, p2 A, k4 MC, [p2 A, k2 MC] 3 times, p2 A.

Row 3: K1 MC, [k2 A, k2 MC] 7 times, k2 A, k1 MC.

Row 4: K1 MC, [p2 A, k2 MC] 7 times, p2 A, k1 MC.

Row 5: [K2 MC, k2 A] 3 times, k2 MC, k4 A, [k2 MC, k2 A] 3 times, k2 MC.

Row 6: [K2 MC, p2 A] 3 times, k2 MC, p4 A, [k2 MC, p2 A] 3 times, k2 MC.

Row 7: K1 MC, [k2 A, k2 MC] 7 times, k2 A, k1 MC.

Row 8: K1 MC, [p2 A, k2 MC] 7 times, p2 A, k1 MC.

Repeat Rows 1–8 for Two-Color Zigzag.

NOTES

Take the time to knit a gauge swatch. Not only will it allow you to determine if your stitches are the correct size, it will also give you an opportunity to learn the stitch pattern and acquire the tension necessary for the color knitting. A gauge swatch of the Two-Color Zigzag makes a lovely square. You might even decide to make several of them and sew them together to make another baby blanket.

You may work the Two-Color Zigzag from the Chart or the written pattern.

There are two edge stitches in MC at either end of each row that are worked in Garter stitch (knit every row); you may wish to place markers between these stitches and the Two-Color Zigzag. You may also wish to place markers between the repeats of the stitch pattern. All stitches worked in MC are worked in Garter stitch; all stitches worked in A are worked in Stockinette stitch. When working WS rows, be sure to bring the MC to the front before working purl stitches, so that you do not carry floats across the RS.

Block the Blanket by holding a steam iron over the piece, without touching it.

For a larger Blanket, cast on an extra 32 stitches (one additional pattern repeat). For a wider border, you could add 4 Garter stitch rows to the Blanket's top and bottom and an extra 2 stitches of Garter stitch to both sides. Make sure to purchase additional yarn if you make the Blanket larger.

BLANKET
Using MC, CO 100 sts. Begin Garter st (knit every row); work even for 4 rows.
Next Row (RS): K2 MC [edge sts, keep in Garter st (knit every row)], work Two-Color Zigzag to last 2 sts, k2 MC (edge sts, keep in Garter st). Work even until you have completed 15 vertical repeats of Two-Color Zigzag. Cut A.
Next Row (RS): Continuing in MC, change to Garter st; work even for 4 rows. BO all sts knitwise.

FINISHING
Block to measurements.

THE KNITTING LESSON

EARNING TO KNIT WAS AN UNCEREMONIOUS EVENT FOR me, lost in the jumble of the day-to-day. The yarn and the needles are all I remember. The rose-colored wool, rolled tightly into a ball, was donated by a neighbor. The long green needles, supplied by my mother, were aluminum and hollow, the kind that really do make a click-clack sound. Stamped on the circular metal ends of each one was the number 8.

I was a noisy, spacey kid—a nudnik. I was always talking, always interrupting, always wanting something. Knitting smoothed my rough edges and gave me pause. I wonder if that's why my mother taught me, hoping that my knitting might earn her some restful moments. Now, with children of my own, I can understand this hope.

My oldest daughters are a mere twenty-one months apart. They were the Meera and Flory team—their own private entertainment center. Birth order put my youngest daughter, Lelia, on the periphery of their world. Her sisters mastered pig latin when she was just learning to talk, and they spoke it together so fast only they were able to understand each other. Which, of course, was the point.

Without her sisters to pal around with her, Lelia turned to my husband, Rody, to fill the gap. He and Lelia chased balls, swam, and regularly visited the Minnesota Zoo and the Children's Museum in St. Paul. In the summer, she rooted for him at his Sunday morning tennis matches. Rody kept a portable checkers set in his car so that when the spirit moved them, they could play over hot chocolate at our local java joint.

When Rody was unavailable for fun and play, Lelia looked to me. I wasn't as active as Rody, so our time together was more like a never-ending tea party. Lelia loved good food and conversation. She had a million questions, a vast number of opinions, and an extensive repertoire of stories to tell and songs to sing.

Charming and lovable, Lelia too was a demanding, nudniky little kid. A minute alone for contemplation and reflection seemed to signal to Lelia that I needed company. A short break to read or knit was always intruded upon by her enthusiasm. When she turned seven, I decided it was time for her to learn to knit. I was sure it would settle her down a bit. It had worked for me.

I had visions of us knitting companionably in our orderly living room, strains of an Irish ballad in the background. Lelia might hum along contentedly while I concentrated on the lace pattern of a Shetland shawl. If she wasn't absorbed in counting her own stitches or rows, we might chat a bit. Time would pass peacefully, in a knitterly way.

Preparing for this life-changing lesson, I read articles on how to teach children knitting, underlining and taking notes. I found a lot of good advice, complemented by great stories and heartwarming anecdotes. I couldn't remember my own first knitting lesson, but I was determined that Lelia's would be unforgettable.

Inspiring materials were important, I believed. So I purchased child-sized wooden needles with ladybugs on the ends and a soft skein of rainbow-colored hand-dyed merino wool. No hand-me-down yarn and clumsy, click-clacking needles. The big event was planned for a Saturday afternoon when the rest of the flock would be out of the house.

When the afternoon of the knitting lesson came, we sat side by side on the living-room couch, our knitting baskets on the floor. Like religious Jews, who start their young scholar's first day with a taste of honey, our coffee table was set with treats to ensure Leila's knitting life a sweet beginning. After the tea and cupcakes, I planned to show her the knitting basics, in poetry and gesture. But I never got that far.

"Mom," Lelia said right after I began, "I think I already know how. I've been watching you."

She nodded toward the needles in my hands—her needles. Confidently, she took hold. Expertly, she knit stitch after stitch.

"See?" she said, lifting her work up high. She beamed at me. Her two front teeth were missing. Her skin was seven-year-old perfect—like her first stitches.

The early afternoon light shone through the living-room window as she knit. A wind scattered a sheaf of leaves, causing a shadow or two to cross the room. On the sidewalk outside, kids were jumping rope, chalking up the sidewalk, and scootering around. It was a glorious fall day, and eventually, knitting just couldn't compete.

Lelia stitched a few more rows while I sipped my tea and watched. Then she put the yarn and needles down on top of the plate of cupcakes and briefly examined the crumbs on her sweatshirt.

"Can I go now?" she asked me.

"Sure," I said. The lesson was over.

With a quick good-bye, she was out the front door, giving me time for contemplation and reflection. I poured myself another cup of tea.

Osmosis: the gradual, often unconscious, absorption of knowledge or ideas through continual exposure rather than deliberate learning. Lelia didn't need the ladybug needles or even the special afternoon to learn to knit. She had learned by osmosis. Is that why I don't remember my mother teaching me? Because I already knew?

After Lelia left the knitting lesson, I wished I could have called my mother, but she had died years before my children were born. Even though I was pretty sure I knew how and why she had taught me to knit, I yearned to hear it from her.

I cleared our dishes, leaving the hand-dyed yarn and oh-so-cute child-sized needles out for Lelia in an inviting tableau. It had taken me time to join my mother in knitting, I remembered. I would wait for Lelia, I thought then, as I imagined my mother had waited for me to emerge from a noisy, nudniky cocoon and find the quieting comfort of knitting. Lelia is a teenager now, and it's the clarinet that has called out to her and focused her energy. To my delight, many evenings I knit while listening

SAFE RETURN

BY CATHERINE DEXTER

Safe Return, a middle-grade novel named after a Swedish mitten pattern, is one of my absolute, hands-down, all-time favorite children's books. A beautiful and moving tale, *Safe Return* takes place in the stark setting of Sweden's Gotland Island. The main character, Ursula, an orphan from the mainland, is being raised there by her aunt and uncle. Her outsider feeling is reinforced by her inability to knit, a skill acquired early by the other children in Visby, their fishing and farming village.

Many books for kids that involve knitting are about the process. In *Safe Return,* the character learns not only how to knit, but how knitting can soothe even a reluctant knitter's turbulent times. There is an authentic tenderness to the text that reflects the author's understanding of the setting, character, and knitting. You can almost feel the lanolin in newly spun wool, the fierceness of the wind, and the darkness of the night in a time and place before electricity. And in *Safe Return,* you will experience the joy that comes in a very satisfying ending.

to her practice, her music surrounding me, the whole room charged with lush sounds. Every so often, when she's finished, she plops herself down in one of our big armchairs, chatting like she did when she was small about anything and everything, providing grand company.

A lot of parenting is about pointing. Here are the needles. Here is the yarn. And here is the chair where I sit knitting. Children grow up, venture forth, and discover their own comforts and joys. Next year, Lelia will leave home for college. I no longer know where I stored the ladybug needles and rainbow wool I bought to bring her into my knitting circle, but I still hope that she'll return to join me there one day.

FOOLPROOF FROSTING

For cupcakes, I place my faith in Betty Crocker. Her cake mixes rarely disappoint and allow me to focus on what to me is most important—the frosting.

1 stick (½ cup) unsalted butter
2 teaspoons vanilla extract (see Note)
Approximately 4 cups powdered sugar
Approximately 2 tablespoons milk

In a medium saucepan or in the top of a double boiler over medium-low heat, slowly melt butter; watch carefully and if butter begins to brown, lower heat.

Remove saucepan from burner and add vanilla. One heaping tablespoon at a time, stir in the powdered sugar until mixture is very thick and stiff. Add milk, ½ tablespoon at a time, until frosting is shiny, smooth, and easy to stir. Let sit for about 10 minutes, then test consistency. If it is too thick, add more milk, 1 teaspoon at a time; if it is too runny, add more sugar.

Makes 4 cups. Store in refrigerator.

NOTE: If desired, substitute peppermint, almond, or maple extract for the vanilla. To make chocolate frosting, add 2 tablespoons unsweetened cocoa powder with the powdered sugar.

Tips for a
Successful Frosting
Experience

- Let your cupcakes or cake cool before frosting. When ready, using a frosting spreader, apply a thin "primer coat" of frosting, wait about 10 minutes, then apply a second coat. If your first coat is bumpy with crumbs, don't worry. Your second coat is your concealer.

- Give extra zip to your confections by adding sprinkles, miniature M&M's, or mini marshmallows on top of the frosting.

- If you want a palette of colors, divide the frosting into small containers. Add food coloring, working it in drop by drop, until you have the color you need.

- Sandwich leftover frosting between graham crackers for a delicious treat.

PLAYTIME CAPE
A PROJECT TO KNIT TOGETHER

M AYBE I NEEDED MORE THAN THE LADYBUG NEEDLES and rainbow yarn to lure my youngest daughter, Lelia, into a love of knitting. What if I had shown her a fun project like this cape that we could have made together? And what if she had needed only to contribute a couple of stitches, or rows, for every few inches I knit on it and could have made the tie on a knitting spool and extra pom-poms (that can be used to hide mistakes) with a pom-pom maker?

SIZE
One size fits most children ages 3–10

FINISHED MEASUREMENTS
21" wide at bottom edge x 17" long

YARN
Lion Brand LB Collection Superwash Merino (100% superwash merino; 306 yards / 100 grams): 1 skein each #114 Chili (MC) and #170 Dijon (A)

NEEDLES
One pair double-pointed needles (dpn) size US 8 (5 mm)
One 29" (70 cm) long circular (circ) needle size US 10 (6mm)
Change needle size if necessary to obtain correct gauge.

NOTIONS
Stitch markers; medium-size knitting spool (sometimes called a French knitter; optional); ¾" and 1" pom-pom makers (optional)

GAUGE
16 sts and 32 rows = 4" (10 cm) in Garter stitch (knit every row)

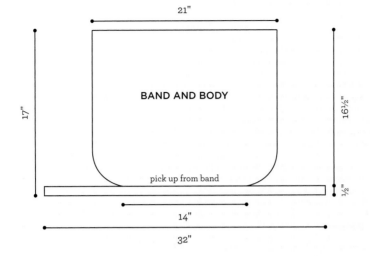

21"

17"

BAND AND BODY

16½"

pick up from band

½"

14"

32"

NOTE: *Piece is worked from the top down.*

NOTES

This Cape is designed to be worked as a cooperative project. The I-Cord Band is quick and easy for a child to work using a knitting spool; make sure that the Band is not worked too tightly. If you prefer, you or the child may work the I-Cord Band without using a knitting spool (see below). The increase rows in the Body of the Cape are intended for the adult to work, but they could be worked by a skilled child knitter. The plain rows in between and at the bottom portion of the Cape should be easy for beginning child knitters.

The Pom-poms can be made using a pom-pom maker or by following instructions given in pattern. Place them in a pattern of your choice, or use them to cover knitting mistakes.

BAND

Using MC and knitting spool (optional), work I-Cord 32" long.
NOTE: If you prefer to work I-Cord without using a knitting spool, see Special Techniques, page 158. Place st marker 9½" from each end of Band.

BODY

Using MC and circ needle, pick up and knit 56 sts between markers. Begin Garter st (knit every row); work even for 1 row.

Shape Body

Next Row (RS): Continuing in Garter st, increase 1 st each side this row, then every other row 13 times, as follows: K1, k1-f/b, knit to last 2 sts, k1-f/b, k1—84 sts. Work even until piece measures 17", or to desired length from the beginning, including the Band. BO all sts knitwise.

FINISHING

Lightly block.

Pom-poms

Using A, make desired number of ¾" and 1" Pom-poms. You can use a pom-pom maker or the following method: Holding middle and forefingers close together, but not touching, wrap yarn around both fingers about 50 times, making sure not to wrap yarn too tightly. **Note:** Wrapping adult fingers will give you approximately 1" Pom-poms; wrapping children's fingers will give you approximately ¾" Pom-poms.

Cut yarn. Cut additional strand of yarn 12" long for tie. Thread one end of tie between fingers, closer to palm, and the other end between fingertips, making sure the strand wraps around all the wrapped strands. Tie a single knot as tightly as possible, then slide the wrapped Pom-pom off the fingers and tighten the knot, adding a second knot to secure. Cut through all the looped ends. Fluff the Pom-pom strands until you have a ball. Trim the ends so that the ball is even all around, making sure not to trim the tie strands.

Using ends of tie, sew Pom-poms evenly spaced around bottom of Body, placing first and last Pom-poms 1½" in from front edges, and approximately 1–2" from bottom edge, staggering location and size of Pom-poms, as desired (see photo).

BUT SHE DOESN'T HAVE
ANY UNDERPANTS

"Success is a function of persistence and doggedness
and the willingness to work hard for twenty-five
minutes to make sense of something that most people
would give up on after thirty seconds."
—Malcolm Gladwell, *Outliers*

J UST ABOUT EVERYTHING I KNOW ABOUT KNITTING FOR others, I've learned from my family. They've showed me what happens when a pattern meets a person. They've educated me in color refinement and yarn selection. They've sent me off for advanced training in pattern customizing.

Let's start with my oldest daughter, Meera.

The idea, probably found in a now-defunct parenting magazine, was that there should always be a handmade gift included in your child's haul of birthday gifts. So for Meera's fifth birthday, I knit her a doll. With golden brown skin, she had thick, wooly black hair, and she wore what I was sure would tickle Meera most, a glamorous rainbow dress crocheted from rich cotton chenille.

"I love her!" Meera told me. Then she turned the doll upside down, checking for critical components. "But she doesn't have any underpants."

Right away, from some leftover pink baby yarn, a petite pair of panties was crafted. Naively, I thought I was done.

"She doesn't have long hair you can braid," said Meera as she pulled her doll's panties on. To get this right I called my friend Monica Leo, a puppeteer and doll maker, in Iowa. Lengths of black wool were added and, when braided, exposed the doll's ears—and another flaw.

"She doesn't have any earrings," exclaimed Meera. A few beads were firmly secured.

When her doll got Mary Janes with silk ribbon roses and Velcro straps, she passed her final test. Meera taught me to consider my knitting a work in progress, and to appreciate details—because a glamorous dress just isn't enough.

Love pushes a knitter's needles—my needles—to create the best we can for our family. And we click on, anxious to see their enchantment with what we have crafted just for them. When snow is anticipated, we knit past our bedtime to finish a hat. Our love for them sends us searching for the best ways to provide for their warmth and comfort, which brings me to my middle daughter, Flory.

As a toddler, once settled in her car seat or stroller, Flory would pull off her pink mittens, hand-me-downs from Meera and hand-knit by me. Her sweet little hands were chapped. Desperate to keep them covered, I knit her mittens as cuddly as the stuffed animals she adored, in red angora with a strand of yellow carried behind each stitch, for double softness and warmth.

Did she keep those masterpieces on? Of course not. Ditched, shed, and dropped, they never stayed put. Finally admitting defeat, I compromised by taking hand-knit blankets along on our outings. Snuggling up with them protected her hands.

Now, one of those angora mittens is lost forever. For many years, the other stayed safe in our hope chest. But when Flory was in high school, I discovered it hanging on the wall by her bed. The sight of it convinced me that, from time to time, the things you knit may have a higher calling, and your deepest hopes for them can come true—just not in the way you envisioned.

Now there's daughter number three: my youngest, Lelia.

Do you know the story of the princess and the pea? Well, Lelia is that type of princess. If there's a tiny knot, a trace of bulk, a fit that's not near perfect, it will be noticed, and the knitted gift will never be worn. Yarns with a scratch factor need not apply. Lelia has taught me to be careful: to take the time to get my gauge right, to measure early and often, to choose yarns well, and to consider finishing a crucial step.

Finally, meet my husband, Rody.

He is how I know that not everyone covets a pair of handmade socks and cable-knit sweaters. His sheer happiness with hats and mittens has kept our marriage safe from knitting conflicts. A missed rib, a backwards cable, an unintended variation in design—those mistakes, Rody assures me, are not likely to be noticed and never affect warmth. If it goes over the head, covers the ears, or slips on the hands, it's a keeper.

And so my homeschooling education continues. There's a lot left for me to master, but I've been a good student, and I have a few things down pat. Like knowing that knitting for family must be a collaborative project. Or realizing that success comes from understanding each member's needs and wants. The doll that gets loved, the socks that wear out from constant use, the hat that's grabbed every time a loved one braves the cold—those are the gold stars you earn. Accepting rejection of your knitterly love is the hardest lesson to master. But take heart, life is full of wonderful surprises, and sometimes our greatest rewards come later, like catching a glimpse of a toddler's mitten enshrined on a teenager's wall.

MY MOTHER,
LILLIAN EDWARDS

"No song or poem will bear my mother's name.
Yet so many of the stories I write, that we all write,
are my mother's stories."
—Alice Walker, *In Search of Our Mothers' Gardens*

M Y MOTHER, LILLIAN EDWARDS, WAS A LIFELONG KNITTER. She was an attractive, well-dressed woman: tall and thin with black hair and almond-shaped brown eyes that almost looked Asian. She called them "laughing eyes," and that is how I like to remember them.

I'm told that as a young woman, my mother knit argyle socks. It was in the days before I was born, perhaps before she was married. Maybe it was when she was a young single woman working in Manhattan and living with her parents in their tiny apartment on Mermaid Avenue in Coney Island.

My mother grew up poor. Her parents were both Russian immigrants. My grandma Yetta, a simple woman, never knew her real birthday. She wasn't even sure of the year she was born. She was a child when she left Russia sometime around the turn of the century, but she never adjusted to America, especially urban life. She never learned how to ride a bus or a subway. She suffered from migraines and rested a lot. She wrapped a handkerchief soaked in vinegar around her head to ease her pain.

I knew my grandfather Samuel, her husband, as a quiet and gentle man, but he had actually been a gangster during Prohibition. When his brother was gunned down in broad daylight, my grandparents fled their home in Philadelphia, taking my mother and my uncle to Coney Island, where they melded into the mass of Russian Jews who lived there.

I don't know who taught my mother to knit. Maybe my grandmother did, when she was not resting. I never thought to ask my mother when she was alive. I know that she taught me to knit and that she knit like a Russian Jew, with her yarn in her left hand, wrapped around the second finger, picking open the stitch and pulling the yarn through with her right-hand needle. It's a fast and efficient way to knit, and I am often asked by knitters out here in the Midwest to teach them "my way" of knitting.

My mother's knitting was like her "laughing eyes," a part of who she was. By the time I knew my mother as a knitter, she was a middle-class housewife and bought her yarn at Pearl's Yarn Store in Troy, New York, where we lived. She purchased her yarn sensibly, project by project. No large stash of "one day I might use this" yarn.

Pearl Berg had a store in a brick building next to the gas station that her husband, Art, owned. There was a picture window in front and an awning outside shading the word PEARL'S. Inside the store was a wooden table covered with knitting projects and floor-to-ceiling cubbies of yarn.

The yarn in those cubbies was made into beautiful sweaters by my mother. At the height of the acrylic craze, my mother knit with wool. She knit lots of mittens, even kitten ones with googly eyes. She made hooded ski sweaters for the three of us kids to wear, and a very large tennis sweater for my very large father, who never played tennis. She knit a stunning green mohair and silk car coat for herself, even though she didn't learn to drive until later in life. She knit mohair sweaters for me and my sister. Mine was cream colored with specks of yellow and blue and red. My sister, the blue-eyed exception in our brown-eyed family, had a baby-blue version with a navy cable up the center. I remember getting to choose the yarn and my mother taking our measurements. I remember trying on the sleeveless sweater. And most of all, I remember my mother's solid advice: When you knit a sweater, do both sleeves at once.

As my mother grew older, Pearl's went out of business. She bought her yarn where she could, mostly W. T. Grants, the discount store in the new shopping plaza not far from our house. She began to knit easy projects, like the "Florida sweater" she learned to knit when she was visiting my aunt and uncle there. With lots of dropped-stitch rows and no shaping, it knit up in a flash. She started to pick variegated acrylic yarns, and she crocheted afghans instead of knitting. We kids were all gone by then, my father died young, and, alone in an empty house, my mom would crochet in the evenings. Mindless handwork while she mindlessly watched TV. It could have been the tumor that eventually and slowly took over her brain or the overwhelming sadness of being alone, but the zip went out of my mother's knitting in those years.

The last project my mother ever did was one we crocheted together: a simple afghan, starting as a rectangle and with colors changing every couple of inches. We used black to mark the color changes, and whenever I came home from Iowa, where I was in graduate school then, I would work on it, too. It is the only piece of my mother's handwork that I still own. It is very large and heavy, almost like a rug. I am amazed that my mother and I, two pretty good knitters, would think to crochet such a clunky piece. But we did. It tied us together in a way that has brought warmth to the grandchildren she never met. They love that afghan, and it was crocheted so tightly that it should be around to warm the next generations. And for the other legacy of my mother's knitting, the competent and careful, there is me.

My oldest daughter, Meera, has my mother's "laughing eyes." She and her two sisters have my mother's sense of fashion and style. Letting them choose their own yarns and patterns, I knit for them the way my mother once knit for me. Sometimes I even use her needles: long white plastic circulars from Pearl's. And if I knit them a sweater, yarn in my left hand, stitches picked open with my right, I always make both sleeves at once.

THE MEMORY SKEIN

"Don't lose the colors that open paths for you
in your small walled garden this afternoon. Look.
Here they are. Touch them. They are the same colors
that live in your heart, a little faded now."
—Raphael Alberti, "Going Back Through Color"
(translated by Mark Strand)

MANY NAMES CIRCLE AROUND THIS COLOR. MY FAVORITE is "Underappreciated Green." It's not quite a sage, a khaki, or a chartreuse. Mixed from blue, with lots of yellow, brown, and white, it's the color of a yarn that lives in my heart, the green of the mohair my mother used to knit herself one of those car coats women wore in the 1960s. When she died in January 1984, I inherited it.

After her funeral, I returned with her car coat to Iowa City, where I was finishing graduate school. With a wide collar and deep pockets, it was a classic. And better yet, it was a perfect fit. I wore it in the spring after her death. Often. People would stop and ask me about my unusual hand-knit coat. That gave me an opportunity to talk about my mother, the one she had been before the last months of her illness, when brain cancer devastated and diminished her. My smiling, knitting mother, who had a wonderful sense of style and color, who loved people, and who was a good friend to many. That's how I wanted to remember her.

March comes in like a lion and goes out like a lamb. Or so the saying goes. But out here on the prairie, some years we jump right over the lamb part. Cold spring weather can turn hot quickly, even from one day to the next. And so when the cold shifted swiftly that spring, I must have shed my mother's coat absentmindedly. My life was crowded at that time, as I was trying to finish graduate school, work part-time, and maintain my increasingly serious relationship with Rody. It wasn't until the fall that I realized the coat was lost.

For almost a decade, that coat lived on in my heart. Rody and I had married, moved to St. Paul, and become parents of three girls when I chanced upon a green mohair yarn, an almost perfect match to the yarn my mother used for her coat. I bought three skeins, two solid green ones and another stranded with magenta, purple, and bright green silk. A pair of super-warm mittens for my middle daughter, Flory, was knit from the two solids. The last skein remained unknit, infused with my memories of my mother. When I opened the dresser drawer where it was kept, the yarn always held me there, bidding me to finger the softness and delivering to me something prized from the storehouse of all that was my mother: a piece of advice given and ignored, a saying she favored, a hairstyle she wore.

When Rody and I moved with the kids back to Iowa City, the memory skein moved, too. The yarn, no longer available, had aged into a talisman, too dear to ever use.

On one of our first days in our new house, while checking the local phone book to see if any of his old tennis buddies were still in town, Rody discovered a listing for Zeke and Irene Palnick. As a young AmeriCorps VISTA volunteer in Arkansas, Rody had been friends with a Zeke and Irene Palnick. Zeke was a Little Rock rabbi back then, and he and Irene, activists in the Civil Rights movement, shared Rody's commitment to social justice. They opened their house to him, inviting him there for meals and holidays. More than a decade younger than they were, Rody babysat their children, Rachelle and Lazar. And he and Zeke golfed together. Over the years, I often sympathized with Rody's regret that he had lost touch with them. Calling the number immediately, he was overjoyed to learn that they had also moved to Iowa City. It wasn't long before we all became friends.

Zeke wasn't well. And just a few years later, at the age of seventy, while wintering in Florida, he died. It was a great loss. I brought some mandel bread to Irene, who loves Rody's mother's recipe. But I wanted to do something more for her, offer a more enduring solace—like a shawl.

Irene loves colors, and she has a bohemian style of dressing. I knew the perfect yarn for her shawl: my memory skein. I had never planned to use it; its transporting powers were still strong. But Irene is a kind, generous, and admirable friend. Knitting for her with it would be like sharing my mother, like entrusting her to the trustworthy.

A luxurious yarn, there was probably less than one hundred yards of it, not quite enough for a shawl. Carefully, painstakingly, I separated the green mohair strand from the silk, doubling my yardage. Casting on with the green, and then alternating between the two yarns every other row, I knit until it all was gone. I found a gorgeous purple silk-wool blend and continued with that, and when that was gone, I bought a hot pink eyelash yarn and edged the entire shawl. My mother never would have worn anything like this, but Irene would. My finishing touch was a loopy border crocheted over the eyelash edging with a burnt orange of the same silk-wool blend.

Rody and I drove the shawl right over. Usually my knitting evokes a very limited response from him, but this shawl was different. It had touched him. He insisted on bringing a camera with us, and he took several pictures of it—pictures I still have.

Irene put her shawl on during our visit that evening in the spring of 2005. While we were there, she never took it off.

"About the shawl," Irene wrote me recently from her winter home. "It has become part of my personality and accompanies me almost everywhere I go here in Florida and on my travels. It wraps around me and gives me warmth and love—and introduces me to many new people, because many people ask me where I got it and seem to want to be included as part of it."

I do believe that my mother's loving spirit, her friendly smile even, was knit into Irene's shawl, keeping her company when she wears it. Believing that is what helped me part with that skein, sliding it from my heart onto Irene's shoulders.

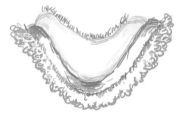

SIS GESSNER'S MANDEL BREAD

My husband's mother, Florence, or "Sis" Gessner, was a great baker who learned her craft working at her father's Pittsburgh bakery from 1930 until 1939, the year she married the accountant who kept the bakery's books. We have inherited all their recipes. This is one of the simplest—and most delicious.

2¾ cups all-purpose flour
1 cup granulated sugar
1 cup ground almonds (see Note)
¾ cup canola oil
3 large eggs
1 teaspoon pure vanilla extract
1 teaspoon pure almond extract

Preheat oven to 350°F. Line a cookie sheet with parchment paper or silicone pan liners.

In a large mixing bowl, combine the flour, sugar, and ground almonds. In a separate, smaller bowl or large measuring cup, combine the oil, eggs, and vanilla and almond extracts, then stir the liquid mixture into the flour mixture until it forms a thick, doughlike batter. Alternatively, this can be done in a food processor or stand mixer with dough attachment. With wet hands, form the dough into two logs about 11½" long, then flatten and shape them so they are about 2" wide and about ½" high.

Bake 25 to 30 minutes, until tops are light golden. Remove cookie sheet from oven, cut each log into approximately ¼" to ½" slices, then place the slices flat-side down on cookie sheet. Reduce oven temperature to 300°F, return mandel bread to oven and bake for about 20 minutes, or until dry and golden.

Makes about 40 mandels.

Note: I like to toast my almonds before grinding them. If you have extra ground almonds, you can roll the logs in them or use them to coat the bottom of the pan. I have successfully added mini chocolate chips, chocolate-covered cherries, poppy seeds, and cinnamon chips to the batter. Sometimes, after slicing the logs, I sprinkle the individual slices with cinnamon sugar.

CHAPTER 2

Home

HERE LIVES A KNITTER

FELL IN LOVE WITH THE CHAIR RIGHT AWAY. UPHOLSTERED IN A deep forest green, with rich mustard, red, and navy stripes, it was the kind of chair I imagined real grown-ups bought. Rody and I had been married for more than a decade. Our three daughters were ages seven, five, and two. We had just moved into a bigger house, complete with a climbing tree in the front yard. No mistaking it, we were adults.

The chair was roomy enough for me, plus a child or two or three, to bond in its coziness with a plate of snacks and a pile of books. There was even a matching ottoman to rest my tired, mature feet on. A second chair, its twin, was available, too. One for Rody. One for me.

"My parents each had their own Barcalounger," Rody told me when I first met him. "Reclining in them, they watched each other grow old and fat."

At the time, this didn't seem a very romantic notion, but when I fell in love that day at Dayton's Furniture Warehouse, we followed this family tradition, snagging the Papa and Mama Bear chairs, and the ottoman. From the moment they entered our lives, these beauties became a treasured part of our living room, and they have continued to be. Our children are now almost adults themselves, and they no longer pile in with us to hear a story. From our thrones, we watch them model their most recent purchases, listen to their stories without us as the main characters, and, on occasion, wait for them to call. A lot of our life happens around our chairs. Usually with us seated in them.

For the most part, the years have been kind to our upholstered friends. They have weathered all sorts of storms and spills unscathed—with one exception. Several years ago, someone—a child someone, and exactly which one is an unsolved mystery—angry about our move from St. Paul to Iowa City, took one of the box cutters that were everywhere during our unpacking days and slashed an ugly slit on the armrest of Rody's chair. Impossible to ignore, it was a strike that hit its mark.

"Can you fix it?" Rody asked, confident that I'd know how.

But I didn't. It was a chair, not a sock. So it stayed untreated, a memorial to our moving traumas long after they had passed.

Over time, friends, family, neighbors, and possibly even Rody, once parked in the wounded chair, all seemed to hearken to a call from a deep, unknown place: Pick at me. And thus, the otherwise generally well-behaved picked at the chair's cut. The slit took on a new life, frayed, and began to gape, revealing parts of the chair better left unseen. First aid of some sort was needed, but what? With college tuition payments, braces, music lessons, and all the various and sundry costs of raising three girls, this chair would not be reupholstered. Or replaced.

As my children became more independent, my role as mom shifted, allowing more time for knitting. My chair in the living room became my favorite place to work. A bag, stuffed mostly with socks, mittens, and hats in various stages of completion, took up residence by the left side, and a small basket containing squares made from leftover sock yarn inhabited the right side. Someday when I had enough of them, each daughter would have an afghan.

"Does it bother you?" I asked Rody one night. "All this knitting stuff everywhere?"

We were sitting in our chairs, the coffee table between us decorated with stitch markers, stray needles, and snippets of wool from knitting past and present.

"I like it," he said without a pause. "It gives the room a homey feel." Being married to a man who thinks that knitting stuff on the floor and table makes a house feel like a home is what ultimately inspired me. Rody's chair didn't have to be made perfect again. It could be embraced for what it was: fabric needing mending. And almost a decade after our move, the bruise from our uprooting was finally kissed and made better, patched with the homemade, handmade feel that my knitting gave the room. Reaching for a sock yarn square from my knitting basket and sewing it over the cut on the armrest didn't take very long.

Our chairs face each other, just like Rody's parents' chairs did in the stories he told me when we were dating. I try to ignore the signs of our aging and expanding bodies. But I do sometimes glance over at the square, to check up on it, to see how it's faring. I'm proud to report it remains a sturdy soldier protecting its turf.

These days, Rody's chair waits for him on his return from traveling, or mowing the lawn. He likes to read in it, with his feet up on the matching ottoman, so comfortable that he often falls asleep. Visitors allowed to sit in his spot may spend a moment or two contemplating the patch on the armrest. But no one picks at what's underneath, and we don't worry much about it. Such injuries can be repaired. I have a basket of squares. In this house there lives a knitter.

A CHAIR FOR MY MOTHER

BY VERA B. WILLIAMS

Most knitting is done sitting down. If you have a designated knitting chair, a good lamp and a knitting bag or basket can join later, all making it easier to finish a sock, or a sweater, or a knitterly patch.

Virginia Woolf taught women about the need for a room of one's own. And Vera B. Williams taught us all about the need for a chair of one's own. In her classic picture book *A Chair for My Mother*, Rosa's mother hasn't a comfy chair to sink her tired body into when she comes home from waitressing. When their coin jar of Mama's tips and Grandma's grocery savings is filled, Rosa and her extended family go shopping for the perfect chair. It's a must-read for knitters and other chair enthusiasts. You might also like the three companion books about Rosa, her friends and family, and Mama's chair: *Something Special for Me*; *Music, Music for Everyone*; and *A Chair for Always*.

UNTANGLING

*"From that day onward, if any traveler on the open
road asked the way to a kingdom that lay east of the sun
and west of the moon, people would answer,
'The way to that kingdom is hard, but if you reach it, you
will find welcome within.'"*
—Mercer Mayer, *East of the Sun and West of the Moon*

n 2005, I committed myself to knitting one hundred
mittens. My oldest daughter, Meera, committed herself to
lobbying tirelessly to have her curfew changed. Nightly
arguments over the unfairness of reporting home at a set
hour mingled with other injustices relating to car keys and appropriate
dress codes. My middle daughter, Flory, had her own list of grievances.
And Lelia, my youngest, was taking notes. Three against two, the odds
were bad enough even when Rody was home. But when he was gone on
work-related travels, as he frequently was that year, they had me dreaming
of peaceful furloughs from the domestic storms surrounding me.

One Sunday, when I had just finished my seventy-second pair of
mittens and Rody had taken an afternoon flight somewhere, I decided to
crack open a skein of hand-dyed fingering-weight yarn. A soft, sensuous

wool, it was full of knitting promise. Just taking the ball band off and seeing the subtle unfolding of my favorite colors, I could feel my heart rate slowing down. I had been saving this treasure, purchased years before with a gift certificate Rody had given me for our anniversary, for a moment just like this one. Winding it was going to be a soul-soothing break from the mitten commitment and my maternal responsibilities, as well as the first step toward knitting the shawl I had promised myself when I bought the wool. It was a fine reward for navigating this far through the best and worst of times with a trio of teenagers.

I don't own a swift, but I do have a set of fine ladder-back chairs. Opening my skeins, sliding them over the back of the chairs, and standing beside them, I wind my wool by hand, the way my mother taught me. It's a mildly aerobic activity. Very social, too. I've wound yarn while my children do their homework at the table or my neighbor sips her coffee. Time spent rolling my own is like courting time. It's time spent getting to know my wooly partner before I knit with it. A knitter's mating ritual, so to speak. A preparation for full engagement.

Feeling stiff from my morning walk, I decided to roll the yarn in the comfort of my armchair, forgoing the wooden chair's back that would keep the skein unsnarled. I would be very careful, I told myself. After all, I was experienced. Heck, I figured, I probably didn't even need a chair back anymore. Certainly I had graduated to the next step.

Holding the end in my hand, with a few loops wrapped around my fingers, I started to roll. It was slow work because of the yarn's fine gauge. With the yarn spread out in my lap, I vigilantly kept the sides of the skein separated, leaving an empty circle in the center. Slowly rolling the wool as if it were on a track, the yarn's rich colors drew me in, Zenlike, and I watched them change from chocolate brown to amethyst to burgundy, until my meditation was interrupted. Lelia came in the room. She wanted to chat. Assured that this would be a genial conversation and not a walk through the minefield of curfews, I listened attentively to her, establishing the necessary eye contact while continuing to gently roll.

EAST OF THE SUN AND WEST OF THE MOON

BY MERCER MAYER

If you enjoy a bit of adventure in your knitting, you might like reading about characters who really do battle trolls, like the once beautiful and spoiled young maiden in Mercer Mayer's 1980 retelling of *East of the Sun and West of the Moon*. War changes her good fortune. The king's army confiscates her father's harvest and livestock. Distraught, he falls ill. Her mother devotes herself to his care. Now forced to be the family's sole

The eye contact was the road to ruin. I knew it would be. And while we chatted, I could already feel a gentle resistance in the yarn, the first sign of trouble. Still I rolled on, recklessly. Then Lelia left to do something else, and I settled back into my winding.

On my lap, the perfect oval of wool had vanished, replaced by what looked like a plate of fine spaghetti, cooked and tossed. I knew well the risk I took when I chose to abandon the safe, reliable chair back, knew that I had further tempted fate when I kept winding while talking, not paying attention and not looking down. My first cursory attempts to reestablish order just deepened the mess. Yet as I thought about the inch-by-inch rescue that lay ahead, a peaceful lightness enveloped me.

Another knitter might have thought this was a catastrophe. And there had been times, I'll admit, when this had happened before, and I

provider, the maiden's "fine clothes became rags and her hands grew rough." Then, in hope of curing her father, she is given a silver cup and instructed by her mother to fill it with "a clear drink of water from the spring" belonging to the South Wind.

Procuring her father's elixir places her on a path where her talents, strengths, and weaknesses are aided and tested by a cast of the magical, including enchanted frogs, frozen creatures, and trolls. She must travel on the backs of unicorns, goats, the Great Fish of the Sea, and finally the North Wind to a kingdom east of the sun and west of the moon, where she is sure not to "find welcome within." There she defeats the troll princess and her good fortune returns, immediately and forever.

There's much to admire in this lavishly illustrated, superbly told tale. And the young maiden's triumphs over incredible obstacles may give courage to knitters engaged in their own wooly struggles. Look for a copy of this classic in your local library.

had cursed my fate. But that day, that year, instead of a tangled tragedy, I saw an enchanted forest just waiting for me to enter. The skein had knotted in ways I had not thought possible. Almost magical. Here was a new challenge. It would require my best concentration, focus, and determination—higher-order skills that often have little value in day-to-day encounters of the adolescent variety.

Teenagers are far more complicated than yarn. They are emotional. Illogical. At least that's how it was at my house. I never felt I could find a clear path with them, but I knew how to work my way out of wooly entanglements. I would struggle a bit with this yarn, but it would never argue with me. The more unraveled, the less there would be for me to do. And with some luck, my mission might even earn me a few hours of quiet time.

In fairy tales, when the maiden daughter is sent on an impossible quest, she receives tools along the way. A stone turns into a magical harp lulling the ferocious giant to sleep. On my quest, a set of slender steel double-pointed needles and a sewing needle would come to my aid. A cup of tea was my elixir.

Pulling the yarn under, over, and through, puzzling out the jumble, I ventured into winding alleys. I used my slender sewing needle to explore knots and double points to pry them open, loosening them wide enough to slip the ball through the center, often gaining five yards of free unencumbered rolling. Defeats were conceding when there was no possible way to unravel further without breaking the yarn. Rubbing together the broken frayed ends of wool in the palms of my hands felted the join. This allowed me to proceed confidently, bridging over what was broken the way the kitchen truces do with cookies still warm from the oven.

My finished ball looked much like any other ball of yarn. The traces of my hard work were impossible to detect. Untangling the skein, opening passages where there had been none, was a singular and vastly underrated achievement. Quick and easy, really, compared to the lifetime of mothering. My parental arguments would continue long after I had rescued my fair skein. But victorious in wool, I was able to resume my old battles, rested. And later, a shawl was knit.

ESTHER RETISH'S SPAGHETTI SAUCE

When I was looking for a good spaghetti sauce recipe, I e-mailed my friend Esther, a busy mother of three and grandmother of seven, because I know most of her recipes have passed many taste tests.

Leave your knots and tangles behind and pull out that big pot, the one marked 8 quarts on the bottom, for this crowd-pleasing recipe.

2 tablespoons extra-virgin olive oil
1 medium onion, chopped
3 – 4 garlic cloves, minced
2 celery stalks with leaves, sliced
4 (14.5-ounce) cans stewed tomatoes
2 (6-ounce) cans tomato paste
8 cups water
2 tablespoons dried mint
2 tablespoons dried basil
1 tablespoon dried oregano
Salt and pepper

In a heavy-bottomed 8-quart saucepan, heat the olive oil over medium heat. Add the onions and garlic and sauté until lightly browned. Add the celery, stewed tomatoes (with liquid), tomato paste, and water, and using a flat wooden spoon, stir to blend the tomato paste and break up the larger pieces of tomato. Add the mint, basil, and oregano. Lower the heat and simmer, stirring occasionally to avoid scorching the bottom of the pot, for 1 to 3 hours or until you are happy with the flavor and thickness. The longer the sauce cooks, the thicker and richer it will become. Season with salt and pepper as desired.

Makes 11 cups.

CLUTCH OF INSPIRATION

MAYBE IT'S THE TEENAGER IN THE HOUSE BATTLING tirelessly for a later curfew, the economy, or even the weather, but some days we can all use a Clutch of Inspiration, a portable case for uplifting quotes, a special photo, delicious chocolates and teas, inspiring talismans, a favorite scent, or other feel-good items. This is an ideal gift for knitting group buddies, dear friends weathering all varieties of storms, and of course, mothers of teenagers.

. . . .

FINISHED MEASUREMENTS
6" wide x 4" high

YARN
Lion Brand Cotton Ease (50% cotton / 50% acrylic; 207 yards / 100 grams): 1 skein #122 Taupe

NEEDLES
One pair straight needles size US 4 (6 mm)
Change needle size if necessary to obtain correct gauge.

NOTIONS
Removable stitch marker; five ½" buttons; assorted buttons and charms for decoration (optional)

GAUGE
20 sts and 29 rows = 4" (10 cm) in Stockinette stitch (St st)

NOTES
When the piece is laid flat, the side edges will be slightly longer than the center section, because of the difference in row gauge between the Garter st edges and the St st section; block piece lightly to achieve a rectangular shape before sewing side seams.

Using Long-Tail CO (see Special Techniques, page 158), CO 30 sts.

Row 1 (RS) and all Odd-Numbered Rows: Knit.

Row 2: Knit.

Row 4: K1, p28, k1.

Row 6: K2, p26, k2.

Row 8: K3, p24, k3.

Row 10: K4, p22, k4.

Row 12: K5, p20, k5.

Row 14: K6, p18, k6.

Row 16: K7, p16, k7.

Row 18: K8, p14, k8.

Row 20: K9, p12, k9.

Row 22: K10, p10, k10.

Row 24: K11, p8, k11.

Row 26: K12, p6, k12.

Row 28: K13, p4, k13.

Row 30: K14, p2, k14.

Rows 32–36: Knit.

Row 38 and all Even-Numbered Rows through Row 64: Work from Row 30 back to Row 4.

Rows 66–70: Knit. Place marker either end of Row 70.

Row 71: K4, k2tog, [k3, k2tog] 4 times, k4.

Row 72: K4, CO 1 st using Backward Loop CO (see Special Techniques, page 158), [k4, CO 1 st] 4 times, k5.

Rows 73–76: Knit. BO all sts knitwise.

Block piece to rectangle 6" wide x 9" long. Fold CO edge to marker. Sew side seams, leaving remaining rows unsewn for top flap. Sew buttons to front, below CO edge, opposite buttonholes. Sew charms if desired.

THE KNITTER AND THE WOODPECKER

"I hope you love birds, too. It is economical.
It saves going to heaven."
—Emily Dickinson in *Letters of Emily Dickinson*,
vol. 2, ed. Mabel Loomis Todd

W INTER: THE TIME OF YEAR THAT WE KNITTERS respond to the needs of those around us. Community drives for hats and mittens grab our attention. Wristers are made for the clarinet player in the house whose hands are cold no matter how high she turns up the heat. Socks, thick and wooly, are cast on for our frozen-footed friends. New mittens are planned for deserving husbands who really didn't mean to lose those complicated Norwegian ones we slaved over last November, checking and rechecking the thumb pattern. This year there's a new fellow on my to-knit list: Woody, the woodpecker who calls my home his home.

It appears that my studios are woodpecker magnets. Or maybe it's my karma. In St. Paul, a busy woodpecker bored pie-plate-sized holes into the wood siding by my studio window. The loud echoing of his diligent drilling gave me migraines. Vinyl siding, put up when the snow was knee high, did the trick there.

My Iowa City studio came with a woodpecker, too. Now that we have been here for a while, I've taken to referring to him as Woody. A downy woodpecker, according to the bird book I bought; petite, with a "short and dainty" bill and salt-and-pepper feathers, sort of like my own hair. The red patch on his head is how I know he's a Woody, not a Woodina.

Last autumn, a very nice man on a scaffold replaced our Woody-damaged cedar siding. We were told that, occasionally, replacing the damaged wood discourages the woodpeckers from returning. But not our Woody. Early on a Saturday morning only a few weeks later, his hammering woke us up.

What do you do with a woodpecker like Woody, an uninvited and destructive guest who just can't take a hint?

"I could get him with a slingshot," said Rody. We were out on our screened-in porch, where he keeps an old tennis racket, his version of a flyswatter. With superb coordination, he keeps the place bug-free.

"Or poison?" he added quickly, seeing that I wasn't keen on stoning Woody. None of Rody's ideas would have gained approval from the Sierra Club—or me. Besides, according to the University of Colorado Extension Service's website, you need a federal permit from the U.S. Fish and Wildlife Service to kill a woodpecker. In addition, they warn, there could be local regulations.

Wasn't there a peaceful way for us to coexist?

"Your house has invaded the woodpecker's natural habitat," my friend Barb informed me. "Your yard used to be woodland." Barb lives out in the country, a gentle woman living as one with the natural world.

"Hang a feeder," she advised. "Attract his attention and redirect his drilling." That sounded reasonable.

At Paul's, our local, independently owned discount store, where you can find a barn heater, apple pickers, and a complete line of Carhartt outdoor clothing, there's an entire shelf dedicated to woodpecker food. Fruit n' Nut Delight, a block of rendered beef suet, cherry, berry, and apple flavoring, almonds, peanuts, corn, and oats caught my eye. Minus the suet, it might be something I'd enjoy eating. For under twenty dollars, I got a carton of ten and a feeder, a coated wire-mesh contraption.

Right away, the Fruit n' Nut Delight did the job. It was discovered not only by Woody, but a slew of his buddies, including a rather ravenous squirrel, whose movements any gymnast would envy. With the feeder up, it was a happy time for our family, Woody, and all the backyard creatures—until the mighty winds that blow here caused the feeder to take flight to parts unknown. And sure enough, with the feeder gone, Woody went back to his old habit in just a few days. The pecking began right up again. To keep Woody happy and away from the siding meant not only replenishing his food a few times a week, but sometimes replacing the feeder as well. We tried to keep up, but occasionally we slacked off, even when Woody reminded us.

This fall, we were granted reprieve in the form of a paper hornet's nest. After the first frost, when the hornets go to wherever hornets go then, and those who stay become free game, I noticed Woody busy drilling at the nest. With some help from a pair of blue jays, it's taken him most of the winter to get at all the hornet remains. Fascinated by the slow eating away at the nest's structure, I've moved my writing desk to better observe their progress. The nest is almost flimsy now, its paper walls exposed from Woody's beak work. Soon enough it will blow away, and Woody will again be knocking at our door, foraging for food. Unless we begin our year-round feeder parade, the careful watch after each storm, our siding will gradually be stripped bare by his efforts.

The nest has given me time to think about a sturdier feeder. My neighbor, Genie, a birdwatcher, suggests that I hang the feed in an empty onion sack. But that's not aesthetically pleasing, especially after the beauty of the paper hornet's nest in its varying stages. The Bauhaus masters taught that design had a place in our everyday life, so what about a hand-knit bird feeder with strong I-Cord straps? It might bounce and jiggle, but barring a tornado uprooting the tree, it could it brave the Iowa winds. And so that is how this week, I found myself knitting for a woodpecker. Woody.

Like Bauhaus designs, where less is more and form follows function, my feeder pattern is simple, like a holey little purse, with lots of yarnovers through which Woody can peck at the feed. Not sure of his color preference, I chose a magenta kitchen cotton, the kind you use to make washcloths, a workhorse fiber. The feeder was finished after two nights of knitting; the feeder's straps were done over my morning cappuccino. And just so Woody knows I like to have fun, I added two long tassels to the bottom.

After loading fresh Fruit n' Nut Delight in the feeder, I bundled myself in a down jacket, slipped on a pair of sturdy Sorels, and headed out to Woody's tree, where the hornet's nest totters. Anchoring the feeder without ceremony, I left my peace offering and headed out for my morning walk.

Later, at my desk, I viewed my backyard wildlife kingdom, covered white with a still-deep snow, marred by deer tracks, and sparkly with a crusty, icy topping. To this stark landscape, the magenta feeder adds color. I rather like it there. I hope Woody does, too.

ONLY WOOL

"The days are long, the years short."
—Annette Mack

O NLY GOOD FRIENDS AND FOOLS KNIT WOOL AFGHANS in the summer, even with air conditioning. But Annette Mack was more than a good friend, she was a wise guide, and if anyone deserved a hand-knit afghan, she did. For more than sixteen years, this devoted mentor had generously shared with me what she knew about nurturing relationships, running a household, and cultivating a community. Now in her eighties, her kidneys had failed, and she was on dialysis.

It was a beastly summer day when Annette called. A special Iowa brand of humid heat that makes corn in the field grow an extra inch. Air conditioners were humming at high levels all over the state. Smart people moved slowly, stayed inside, rested by a body of water. Committed wool knitters were eyeing cotton and investigating the merits of bamboo and inego yarn, made from our own fast-growing corn. They started socks, washcloths, and hats, works that rested on the needles, not on the lap.

"Are you still knitting?" Annette asked, a question only a nonknitter would ask me.

"Sure." Summer knitting, I should have added.

Annette was going to dialysis several times a week. The treatment room where she sat for hours and hours was damp and very cool. To stay warm, she'd been covering herself with an old sweater, which was now falling apart.

"Could you knit me an afghan?" she asked. "In wool, like my sweater?"

"Of course," I said. "Are you sure you want wool?" Looking out into our backyard, through the heat's haze, the grass was browning to crisp dryness.

"Only wool," she insisted. "Like my sweater."

"What about microfleece?" I asked, my fingers ready to punch in an order to L.L.Bean.

"What's that?"

We had met Annette and her husband, Norman, when we first moved to St. Paul. Decades older than Rody and me, they gathered our children and us into their lives. Over the years of our friendship, Annette was always there to lend a caring ear to my mothering issues. She was delighted to step in as family and attend my children's events, like a grandmother. We celebrated holidays with them. She always remembered our birthdays.

Shortly after we moved to Iowa, Annette had begun dialysis, the first sign of her deteriorating health. Living far away and still weighted with the needs of my own flock, I had been able to offer her only phone support. The afghan was my chance to help her as she had helped me so many times. Annette had asked me for something I could do. So what if it was the wrong season for afghan making?

I found some bright blue worsted wool. Not knowing how much I might need to make an afghan, something I rarely knit, I overbought to be safe—probably at least six skeins too many. In the thick of summer, I hosted an abundance of warmth.

The first afghan pattern I tried out was a washcloth pattern. It's the one that's bias knit in garter stitch, starting with three stitches and increasing with a yarn over at the beginning of every row. It was speedy. After a week of serious knitting time, half the afghan was done. But a right triangle weighing at least five pounds was not the light warmth Annette needed. Later, it became a shawl I keep in my studio. I couldn't bear to tear out the work and didn't have to. A wool arsenal, a stockpile, awaited my next attempt.

I wasted a lot of time testing out pattern after pattern. I critically examined each sample, asking myself every time, would Annette be able to lug this around? No. All were too heavy and bulky.

In the meantime, every few days, the phone would ring. The pressure was on.

"Is it finished yet?" Annette would ask. She was cold.

Guilt followed every call. Self doubt trailed behind. What kind of knitter was I? Why couldn't I fill this simple order? I just couldn't seem to get the right pattern.

I dawdled. Dodging guilt and the heat, worrying this over in an air-conditioned Ben Franklin store one afternoon, I passed a wall of microfleece on my way to the sock yarns. Somewhere between the bolts of pastel camouflage and the gold and black Iowa Hawkeye pattern, I had an epiphany.

Annette loved my children. Never very handy herself, she was impressed by Meera's sewing, the simple pants she made for Lelia one winter. The summer before, at another Ben Franklin in Bemidji, Minnesota, where we were vacationing, and where even in summer the evenings are chilly, Meera had bought a few yards of a yellow and orange plaid microfleece. Blanket stitching all around in yellow yarn and adding long tassels in each corner, she had quickly made an attractive cover, warm and lightweight, like the afghan Annette needed. What if Meera made a blanket like that one for Annette? Annette would treasure whatever she received from Meera, even if it wasn't wool.

Happy to oblige, Meera chose a lambswool-white microfleece and pale blue yarn for the edging. Her creation was completed while watching a movie that evening and was sent out first class the next morning. Meera tucked in a short note explaining that she wanted Annette to be warm while her mother, the knitter, slowly stitched her wooly solution.

Two days later, Annette called.

"What Meera made is just perfect." Annette told me. "So now you don't have to finish that afghan."

But I had started to make great progress, and I couldn't abandon my promise. I had finally found a good pattern. A welted rib with a few yarnovers, knit on larger-than-called-for needles, it had airy warmth. Done in strips, perfect for hot weather knitting, it worked up in a flash. I delivered it a few weeks later.

Meera's microfleece blanket became Annette's trusted dialysis companion. I used to wish I had sent her one immediately after she had called. She would have had it for all those weeks when she called asking about my progress, weeks that proved to be among her last. But those calls were always a chance for us to talk about other things as well. They kept her up-to-date with what was happening with my children. And because it was summer vacation, one or more of them were usually around to say hello, and chat a bit with her.

I also believe that Annette knew how hard I tried to knit her the perfect afghan, my final thank-you to her for all that she had given me over the years. I don't regret my knitting procrastination anymore. These days, I'm thankful for the connection it gave us, right up until the end.

THE SETTLEMENT COOKBOOK
The Way to a Man's Heart

COMPILED BY MRS. SIMON KANDER

*"Actually, if I consult a cookbook at all, it is likely to be by
one of those flat-heeled authors like the famous Mrs. Kander."*
—James Beard

If you don't have an Annette Mack in your life, you can find a good guide in Mrs. Simon Kander, who compiled *The Settlement Cookbook.* My mother's 1949 copy, the enlarged and revised edition complete with a signed picture of Mrs. Simon Kander, offers over 3,700 ethnic Jewish, American, German, and Eastern European "tested recipes from the Milwaukee Public School Kitchens, Girls' Trades and Technical High School, authoritative dieticians, and experienced housewives." Thoughtfully included are also hundreds of helpful instructions for running a household, including canning vegetables, making soap, and my all-time favorite, "Directions for Serving Where There Is No Maid."

The Settlement Cookbook, first published in 1901 to benefit the Milwaukee Settlement House, went through forty editions and sold over two million copies. Although it is currently out of print, various versions are available from libraries and used booksellers.

CHAPTER 3

Community

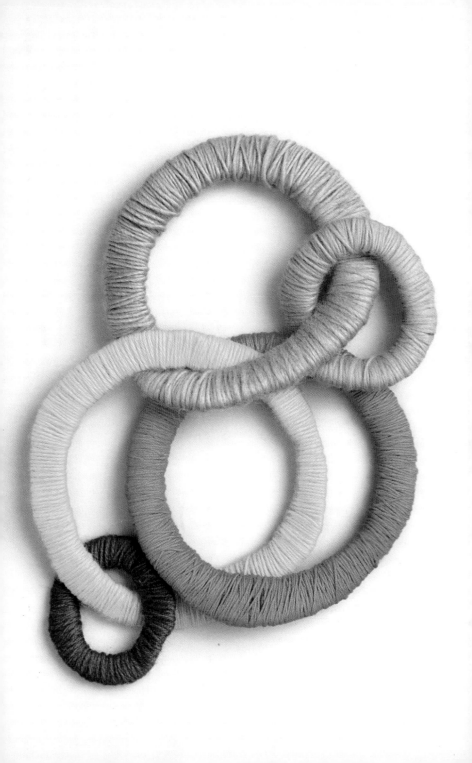

FIRST SOCKS

"What's so miraculous about a spider's web?" said Mrs. Arable.
"I don't see why you say a web is a miracle—it's just a web."
"Ever try to spin one?" asked Dr. Dorian.
Mrs. Arable shifted uneasily in her chair. "No," she replied.
"But I can crochet a doily and I can knit a sock."
—E. B. White, *Charlotte's Web*

NSIDE THE SMALL PLASTIC PACKET WERE FOUR LITTLE skeins of wool: gray, maroon, navy, and gold. Nestled snugly together, they rested on top of the pattern, which was folded over twice to fit neatly. The kit was a relic, most likely from a time before I was born. I had never seen one like it before, nor have I since. Who knew how long it had been in Dora's Yarn Store, tucked away in her narrow cavern of endless cubbies in Albany, New York?

I was eighteen years old that year, 1973, dedicated to pattern-free knitting, fearless and adventurous. An ancient argyle sock kit was not the type of thing I would buy; Dora must have given it to me as a gift for agreeing to take four skeins of navy wool to her sister-in-law in Jerusalem. I was about to leave for six months of work and study on Kibbutz Mizra, taking only one piece of luggage, a frame backpack.

Every item packed was carefully scrutinized. The argyle sock kit was small and oddly intriguing, so in it went. A new kind of knitting for my journey.

On the kibbutz, I lived in a *sarif*, a hut, with two other girls in the program. Our day's obligations usually ended in the late afternoon. After a communal dinner in the kibbutz dining hall, our evening seemed like an endless stretch of possibilities. No TV. No phone calls. My parents had given me a phone credit card I could use in the one phone booth on the kibbutz in case of an emergency, like another war. We wrote letters instead, corresponding on thin blue aerogrammes. Occasionally, we had a little Hebrew homework to do, or there was some organized event. Most evenings, though, were spent visiting with other *ulpanists*, as we were called. Usually I hung out with my Dutch roommate, Mieke, and our friend Jon Zeltsman.

It was amazing how productive those nights were. Talking and drinking tea, I sketched and painted. And in this wealth of time I had to spend as I liked, I opened the sock kit. Sitting on my bed, all the contents of the packet spread out, I was charmed by the fine yarn and curious about how the argyle was knit and the foot was shaped. The kit made me feel as if socks were a doable, fun exercise. With only my own knitting enjoyment in mind, I started my first pair.

Using very skinny, straight needles, and working back and forth, I ribbed a few inches in gray. The argyle was next. Worked in intarsia, each color section required its own yarn supply. Nine bobbins were crafted from spare cardboard. The graph was consulted for the set-up row, and after that, it was no longer needed. The diamonds, and the diagonal lines that intersected them, emerged predictably. Moving from color to color, I twisted the yarns around each other, pulling them extra tight to prevent holes. When I wasn't untangling bobbins, the knitting was fast. As I approached the heel and realized the end was in sight, I began to wonder what I would do with the socks when they were done.

Turning the first heel required me to read that part of the pattern out loud several times. At some point after figuring out short rows, I got a great idea: I'd trade the socks. Because of his woodworking skills, my friend Jon had a permanent job in the kibbutz carpentry shop. I offered to swap the socks for a small lap loom. I wasn't staying forever on the kibbutz, only a few more months, but in my still-adolescent mind, a loom like the one I hoped to get Jon to make me might be a nice thing to have as another evening activity, after the socks were completed.

They were finally finished in the early spring. The argyle was perfect. The heel and toe, too. In fact, each sock was a beauty. I had overlooked only one important detail: the gauge. Turning the heel, keeping true to the argyle, Kitchener stitching the toe—all these fun, new knitting challenges had riveted my attention. The rest of that stuff in the pattern was for knitting wimps—or so I thought.

The socks were way too tiny for Jon—or even me. What's more, he left the kibbutz program early, before the socks were ready. I never got my loom.

I couldn't give the socks away; they didn't fit anyone. And even if they had, no one needed wool socks in spring, when it was already getting very hot in Israel. The socks did not travel home with me; my backpack was loaded with accumulated souvenirs and presents. I hope I didn't toss them, but frustrated with my creation, I might have. I hope that someone, somewhere found them, and has kept them, maybe hanging them on a wall like I do with the abandoned knitting projects that I find in resale shops.

These days, I read a pattern carefully. I want something when all my work is done, something that can be used. From knitting these socks, I learned many things—intarsia, the Kitchener stitch—but mostly, I learned the importance of checking gauge. It is a defining step for knitters in making a garment of any kind. Skipping it reveals intent, the knitter's lack of concern for the fit of the finished item. I know that now.

My first socks were utterly useless. But usefulness wasn't really why I made them. The trade with Jon was just an excuse to vest the time in seeing them finished. The argyle socks with their knitterly hurdles and

CHICKEN MAN

WRITTEN AND ILLUSTRATED BY
MICHELLE EDWARDS

In those long knitting nights on the Kibbutz Mizra, we often told stories. Rodney, another member of my gang of buddies back then, liked to tell about working in the *lul*, the kibbutz chicken coop. There was a chick on the third floor who he claimed was not like any other. Special. All Rodney's chickens were funny and sweet. Irresistible.

Rodney was the model for my picture book character *Chicken Man*, the *kibbutznik* who loves chickens and is loved by them. *Kibbutzim* have changed over the years since I lived there, but as you read *Chicken Man*, you will get a glimpse of the way they were back when I knit my first socks.

hoops were like a crossword puzzle, entertaining to figure out. They were all about process, not product.

It took me many years, almost a quarter of a century, before I made another pair of socks. My hands remembered what I had mastered back when my brain cells were plump and young. My second pair of socks was a utilitarian model, the kind peasant women knit. I was careful to check my gauge and measure my fit often. I have made many socks since, mostly uncomplicated, well-fitting foot apparel. Every so often, for sheer pleasure, I like to try something new: knitting two at time on circulars, toe up, or with a tad of lace. Then I return to my old standards, the pattern I know by heart, the one that will always make a sturdy, practical sock.

There's a place in every knitter's heart reserved for firsts: first scarf, first sweater, first socks. And if I could wander back to the long ago, to Dora's Yarn Store, I'd search through the wooly warrens of her tiny shop until I found a small plastic packet with four little skeins of fine sock wool and a pattern crisply folded. I'd take it straight to my knitting chair. Open it. Spread out the dainty wool. Unfold the pattern. Read it attentively. And before I even started to make the cardboard bobbins, I'd be sure to check my gauge.

JON ZELTSMAN'S ROASTED ROOT VEGETABLES

Writing "First Socks" got me wondering what had happened to Jon Zeltsman. With Google and a few e-mails, we have reconnected, and he even sent me this delicious recipe. I promised him a pair of socks in return—size 8½.

6 cups of any two or three of these vegetables: carrots, parsnips, rutabaga, celery root, or purple-top turnips
2 cups cippolini onions or shallots, halved or quartered
3 cloves garlic, unpeeled, smashed
3 – 4 sprigs fresh thyme
½ teaspoon ground cumin
½ teaspoon ground coriander
Salt and pepper to taste
2 – 3 tablespoons olive oil
2 tablespoons balsamic vinegar
3 tablespoons water

Preheat oven to 350°F. Heat a 13"-by-18" baking pan. Peel and roughly chop the root vegetables into about ½" by 1½" chunks; make all the pieces about the same size so they cook evenly. In a large bowl, combine the chopped vegetables, onions or shallots, and garlic. In a small bowl, combine the thyme, spices, salt, pepper, olive oil, and balsamic vinegar, then pour over the vegetables and stir well.

Pour vegetable mixture onto preheated pan; vegetables should sizzle. Sprinkle with the water. Cover tightly with heavy foil. Roast vegetables for 20–30 minutes, until they pierce easily with a fork. Stir, spreading evenly, then roast another 20 minutes or longer, until caramelized (light brown).

Serves 4–6

QUICK AND EASY
FIRST SOCKS
AKA GUSSIES

FOR YOUR FIRST SOCKS, CHECK YOUR GAUGE EARLY AND often. And even if you are offered a nifty vintage kit like the one Dora gave me, do not mess with argyle. Instead, try these well-fitting Quick and Easy First Socks, which I've nicknamed Gussies because the heel is made like a mitten's thumb gusset. In fact, until you begin the short rows and turn the heel, you can still change your mind and make the Quick and Easy Mittens (aka Pearl; see page 121) instead.

Gussies, which don't have a heel flap or picked-up instep stitches like many traditional socks, are also fun for experienced sock knitters. Many thanks to Wendy T. Johnson of Wendy Knits, whose post about her gusset-heel sock pattern on Ravelry helped me to see the mitten/sock connection.

SIZES
Child's (Women's Small/Medium, Women's Large/Men's Small, Men's Medium/Large)

FINISHED
MEASUREMENTS
6½ (7½, 8½, 9½)" Foot circumference

8 (9½, 10¼, 11)" Foot length from back of Heel
6¼ (6½, 7, 7¼)" Leg length to base of Heel

YARN
Lion Brand Alpine Wool (77% wool / 15% acrylic / 8% rayon; 93 yards / 85 grams): 1 (2, 2, 2) skein(s) #224 Barley

One set of five double-pointed needles (dpn) size US 8 (5 mm)
Change needle size if necessary to obtain correct gauge.

Stitch markers

15 sts and 22 rnds = 4" (10 cm) in Stockinette stitch (St st)

1x1 RIB
(multiple of 2 sts; 1-rnd repeat)
All Rnds: *K1, p1; repeat from * to end.

Using Long-Tail CO (see Special Techniques, page 158), CO 24 (28, 32, 36) sts. Divide sts evenly among 4 needles [6-6-6-6 (7-7-7-7, 8-8-8-8, 9-9-9-9)]. Join for working in the rnd, being careful not to twist sts; place marker (pm) for beginning of rnd. Begin 1x1 Rib; work even until piece measures 3½", or to desired length from the beginning. Knit 3 rnds.

Increase Rnd 1: *Needle 1:* K6 (7, 8, 9) pm, LLI; *Needle 2:* RLI, pm, knit to end of needle; *Needles 3 and 4:* Knit—26 (30, 34, 38) sts [7-7-6-6 (8-8-7-7, 9-9-8-8, 10-10-9-9)]. Knit 1 rnd.
Increase Rnd 2: Increase 2 sts this rnd, then every other rnd 4 (5, 6, 7) times, as follows: *Needle 1:* Knit to marker, slip marker (sm), RLI, knit to end of needle; *Needle 2:* Knit to marker, LLI, sm, knit to end of needle; *Needles 3 and 4:* Knit—36 (42, 48, 54) sts [12-12-6-6 (14-14-7-7, 16-16-8-8, 18-18-9-9)]. Knit 1 rnd.

TURN HEEL

Note: When slipping sts, slip purl sts purlwise and knit sts knitwise.

Set-Up Row 1 (RS): Work back and forth on 24 (28, 32, 36) sts on Needle 1. Leave remaining sts on 2 needles for instep. K13 (15, 17, 19), ssk, k1, turn.

Set-Up Row 2: Slip 1, p3, p2tog, p1, turn.

Row 1: Slip 1, knit to 1 st before gap, ssk (the 2 sts on either side of gap), k1, turn.

Row 2: Slip 1, purl to 1 st before gap, p2tog (the 2 sts on either side of gap), p1, turn.

Repeat Rows 1 and 2 zero (1, 2, 3) time(s)—20 (22, 24, 26) sts remain.

Next Row (RS): *Needle 1:* Slip 1, pm, k3 (4, 5, 6)

GUSSET

Note: Needles will be renumbered on first rnd.

Decrease Rnd 1 (RS): *Needle 1:* With spare needle, k3 (4, 5, 6), pm, k2tog, k5; *Needles 2 and 3:* Knit; *Needle 4:* Knit to 2 sts before marker, k2tog, sm, knit to end of needle—30 (34, 38, 42) sts remain [9-6-6-9 (10-7-7-10, 11-8-8-11, 12-9-9-12). Knit 1 rnd.

Decrease Rnd 2: *Needle 1:* Knit to marker, sm, k2tog, knit to end; *Needles 3 and 4:* Knit; *Needle 4:* Knit to 2 sts before marker, k2tog, sm, knit to end of needle—28 (32, 36, 40) sts remain. Knit 1 rnd.

Repeat Decrease Rnd 2 every other rnd twice—24 (28, 32, 36) sts remain [6-6-6-6 (7-7-7-7, 8-8-8-8, 9-9-9-9)].

FOOT

Work even until Foot measures 6¼ (7½, 8, 8½)", or 1¾ (2, 2¼, 2½)" less than desired length length from back of Heel.

TOE

Decrease Rnd: Decrease 4 sts this rnd, then every other rnd 3 (4, 5, 6) times, as follows: *Needles 1–4:* Knit to last 2 sts on needle, k2tog—8 sts remain (2-2-2-2).

FINISHING

Cut yarn, leaving 5" tail. Thread tail through remaining sts, pull tight, and fasten off.

HOME EC WORKSHOP & THE MYSTERY OF THE INDIAN SLIPPER

"Every day my grandmother would have coffee with
her group of friends. With and without kids.
And here's the part I love. Sometimes they
met twice a day. This was something that my mother
didn't have. That I didn't have. But something
that I wanted. A community of friends that I saw every day."
—Codi Josephson, co-owner of the Home Ec Workshop

A T 701 NORTH LINN STREET, IOWA CITY, IOWA—MY hometown—Codi Josephson and Alisa Weinstein, knitting group buddies, have created a gathering place, a watering hole, an open studio for folks who like to make things: Home Ec Workshop. That's where this story begins.

You can catch the Home Ec spirit when you open the shop's green door and step into the first of three big rooms, this one stocked with fabric, notions, and buttons so artful they make me wish I sewed.

In the middle room, you can order sweets and savories as well as the usual coffeehouse offerings. The cosmic licorice mint tea is my favorite. From a counter stool, you get a great view of the room: the salvaged school cubbies stuffed with wool, cotton, and silk yarns, the old wooden steamer trunk that doubles as a coffee table, and the red couch circled by chairs. All seating is conveniently located so you can overhear what's happening almost anywhere in the store, enabling you to add your wooly two cents to any discussion that may merit your attention—unless you are already engaged in a deep discussion about books, yarn, child-rearing, tattoos, or dating. The Home Ec gang is multicultural, multigenerational, multi-multi.

The back room is a workshop. Tables are set up for sewing and silk-screening. Classes meet there and handcrafters work there as if it were their own studio.

Home Ec is where I go to discuss a story idea or project pattern. It's where I like to meet friends or knit in good company. It's where we went for first aid when my youngest daughter, Lelia, scorched her homecoming dress just hours before the dance. I have wanted a place like this all my life. Knitting and community, seven days a week.

One Friday, I sat alone with my knitting on the red couch. Alisa, one of the owners, took the chair beside me. Our talk turned to a pair of hand-knit slippers she had bought when she lived in India.

"If I bring them in, could you help me figure out how they were knit?"

"Sure," I told her. I'm not the kind of knitter who can puzzle out patterns, but helping Alisa made me want to be.

After the Farmer's Market the next day, Saturday, my friend Deanne and I stopped by Home Ec with her granddaughter.

"I have the slipper," said Alisa. And in between serving lattes and quiche, she showed it to us.

The slipper resembled a pouch. What was so special about it? "Look," said Alisa, trying it on. The slipper fit like a ballet shoe, clinging to the foot and sporting two delicate bands of eyelets that opened up when worn and a neat little pointed toe. They were darling, and appeared deceptively simple. Oddly, the seam was at the heel, not on the bottom where I expected it to be.

"Shouldn't be too hard," I said with bravado. Plus I had Deanne next to me, an artist who knits and sews, and who thinks spatially.

We folded napkins, sketched diagrams, tried every tool in our collective tool box. A thundering of happy and loud chatter chorused around us. The red couch, the chairs, and the floor space were occupied by men sewing very peculiar animals made from socks, a boy playing, and of course, knitters knitting. Through all this, we kept our focus. How did she, our anonymous Indian knitter, make this?

Alisa was busy with customers. Codi had a birthday party in the workshop area.

"She must have . . ." we kept repeating like a mantra, discarding one theory after another. Finally, Deanne had to leave. She handed me a few of her sketches.

"You sure you want to stay?" she asked. She was my ride home.

"Absolutely," I told her, my needles in hand. I'd figure this out by doing, by knitting. I could walk home.

Alisa had bought several slippers from the piles the knitter had for sale. So they must have been uncomplicated, a folk pattern. In between her hectic Saturday store tasks, she checked in on my slow process.

"Go, Michelle, go!" cheered Codi, the birthday party now over. Her cheers kept me knitting. And unraveling. And reknitting. Still, I didn't realize that I was only at the beginning of the quest.

All week, I tried to decipher what was a small bit of everyday knitting for a woman half a world a way. Working out ideas in the evening, in the mornings I'd share what I had done with everyone at Home Ec over tea. I spent a whole week meeting knitters, making new friends, trying out new knitting techniques, and finding answers in corners of my town previously unexplored. It was a week of understanding just how a person's knitting world can open up when a store like Home Ec appears. Like a magical door in the wall.

Monday's slipper was complex, flawed. But I honestly believed I had nailed a cast-on that gave the slipper a seamless bottom.

"Too complicated," Alisa told me. "And mine doesn't look seamless."

"Why not use a Turkish cast-on?" suggested a voice from the red couch. It was Kenda, a doctoral student in anthropology and a fine knitter.

"That was it," Alisa wrote me later. "I'm absolutely sure, and it makes the pointy toe after the first row."

The cast-on solved, I started a new slipper. It was a lovely early summer night, but visions of bringing an exact replica to Home Ec the next morning kept me indoors. I was so close. Or so I thought. The interesting little eyelets that appeared to be created by yarnovers weren't. A careful study of them revealed a different technique, one that picked up the bar between the stitches, knit it once, and then knit it together with the next stitch. That took an evening. The slipper was shaping up. But did I have it right?

A bit of good knitting karma intervened on Wednesday when my Indian neighbor and her husband walked by my house. She has a dynamite charitable knitting group. Surely she would know this pattern. Why hadn't I called her before?

"My group is meeting tonight. Come, someone there will know."

"Why do you need us?" the women asked me after much clucking about my sample. "You have it." But just before the snacks were served, I felt a gentle poke.

"Let me see this again," said Mahmooda, the woman sitting next to me. She focused on the heel.

"This could be better," she suggested, making a rounded movement over the boxy, square corner.

"But that's how the original was," I told her.

"So why does it have to be exactly like that one?"

Why, indeed?

I stayed long enough to taste some superb strawberry salsa and say my nice-to-meet-yous, my thank-yous, and my good-byes. Then, taking their wise advice and trusting my own instincts, I came up with what I hoped was a better heel.

By Friday, the cast-on, the two rows of eyelets, the heel, and a seamless seam were firmly established. I still hadn't figured out the bind-off. Now accepting that faithful deciphering wasn't necessary, I made peace with a conventional one.

Sunday morning I gathered all my slippers, tried them on, and chose the winner. And in my knitting chair, with Alisa's slipper and mine on one arm, a cup of home-brewed cappuccino on the other, I knit, following what I had done in the chosen slipper and referring occasionally to the original. I wrote down everything I did. Dusty crevices of my brain were cleaned and forced into service trying to explain the quirks of the eyelets. Then I stopped for a moment. The night before, a new bind-off had come to me in a dream. Should I give it the old Home Ec try? A sip of my drink and I was off, needling my way through this gift the night had given to me.

Trying on the slipper, I felt a delicious thrill completely unassociated with my three cups of cappuccino. The eyelets blossomed just like those on the original slippers did. The fit was snug and sleek, and the finished edge looked, well, finished. Like Alisa's slipper.

A goal for Team Home Ec! A knitterly victory! A collective effort had helped me solve the mystery of the slipper and, in the process, humbly contribute a few innovations. Like a better heel and no seams.

Two weeks after receiving my assignment, on a beautiful summer Saturday before Home Ec opened, I sat on the red couch next to Alisa and helped her through the eyelets and bind-off. I'd like to imagine that's how the original slipper pattern evolved. Knitter to knitter. A finger pointing to show how. Needles clicking to show a better way.

HEIDI ANDERSON'S SPINACH, ONION, SUN-DRIED TOMATO, AND FETA QUICHE

Heidi Anderson is the master baker behind Sugar Loving Mama's Baked Goods, the line of cookies, cupcakes, and quiches that keep the knitters at Home Ec happy.

CRUST
1 cup (2 sticks) cold, salted butter, cubed
1 cup unbleached all-purpose flour
¼ teaspoon salt
About 3 tablespoons ice water

FILLING
1 tablespoon canola oil
1 bunch green onions, diced
4 cups fresh spinach, chopped
4 ounces feta cheese, crumbled
¼ cup sun-dried tomatoes (dried, not packed in oil), diced
3 large eggs
2 cups half-and-half
½ teaspoon salt
Pepper to taste

To make crust, in a medium mixing bowl and using a pastry cutter, cut the butter into the flour and salt, until the dough looks like small pebbles or coarse sand. Sprinkle in the ice water and, using your hands, incorporate into the dough, making sure there are no lumps of butter. If dough is not holding together, add more water, 1 tablespoon at a time. Preheat oven to 400°F.

Press dough into a circle on a floured surface and roll out to a diameter of about 13". Transfer dough to 9" pie tin and crimp edges. Place another lightweight pie tin on top of it, and put both in freezer for about 15 minutes or until oven is ready, whichever is longer. Bake crust with the extra tin for 10 minutes. Take tins out of oven and reduce heat to 350°F. Remove tin that is resting on top of crust and set aside crust tin on wire rack to cool while making filling.

To make filling, heat canola oil in a medium sauté pan over medium heat. Add green onions and sauté for 3 to 5 minutes, until soft. Add spinach and cook until wilted, about a minute, then remove from heat.

Sprinkle feta cheese on prepared pie crust. Sprinkle sun-dried tomatoes on top of feta. Top with spinach mixture.

In a medium-size bowl, whisk together eggs, half-and-half, salt, and pepper, then pour on top of spinach mixture.

Bake at 350°F for about 30 minutes, until quiche has a custardlike consistency when jiggled. The center should be the same consistency as the edges; it should not slosh when jiggled. Cool for 30 minutes before serving.

Serves 6.

GOOD KARMA SLIPPERS

Once the mystery of the Indian slipper was solved, I wrote this pattern. There are some techniques here that might be new to you, but don't let that stop you, because they're all easy to learn. These slippers are so comfortable that you'll probably want to wear them around the house and take them with you when you travel.

....

SIZE
Women's Small/Medium (Large/X-Large)

FINISHED MEASUREMENTS
7½ (8½)" Foot length from back of Heel
NOTE: Slippers are meant to fit closely and will stretch when worn.

YARN
Lion Brand LB Collection Cotton Bamboo (52% cotton / 48% bamboo; 245 yards / 100 grams): 1 skein each #098 Magnolia (MC) and #102 Cherry Blossom
NOTE: Each skein makes 2 pair.

NEEDLES
Two 16" (40 cm) long circular circ needles size US 5 (3.75 mm) Change needle size if necessary to obtain correct gauge.

NOTIONS
Removable stitch marker

21 sts and 32 rows = 4" (10 cm) in Stockinette stitch (St st)

ABBREVIATIONS

ME (make eyelet): With the tip of the left-hand needle inserted from back to front, lift the strand between the 2 needles onto the left-hand needle; knit the strand through the back loop; slip the resulting st back to the left-hand needle; k2tog-tbl.

NOTES

Turkish CO: Make a slipknot and place it on a circular needle (needle A). Hold a second circular needle (needle B) above the first. Bring the working yarn from the back of A, behind and over B to the front, then under A to the back again. Continue in this manner, wrapping the yarn around both needles so that you have half as many wraps as the number of stitches required for your cast-on. Slide A to the right so that the wraps are now on the cable of the needle, and both ends of the needle are dangling. Using the free end of B, knit the first wrap on the tip of B, making sure that when you knit it, the yarn is coming from under A. Knit all the wraps on B, then rotate both needles together clockwise so that A is now the back needle, and the working yarn is coming from underneath the right-hand end of B. Slide B to the right so that the wraps are now on the cable of the needle, and both ends of the needle are dangling. Slide A to the left so that the wraps are now on the tip of the needle. Slide the slipknot (the first loop on A) off A and pull out the knot. Using the free end of A, knit all the wraps on A, making sure that when you knit the first st, the yarn is coming from under B.

Working in the Round on Two Circular Needles: When you finish working the cast-on, you will be ready to begin the first round. Slide the stitches that you will be working to the tip of the needle; slide the stitches you are not working to the cable of the needle that they are on. With the free end of the needle that holds the stitches that you will be working on, work across those stitches as instructed (Needle 1), making sure to pull the yarn snug when working the first stitch, so that you do not have a gap between it and the last stitch on the other needle. Once these stitches have been worked, slide the needle so that the stitches are on the cable of the needle. Turn the work so that Needle 1 is now in the back, with the working yarn at the right. Slide the other needle (Needle 2) so that the stitches are on the tip of the needle closest to the working yarn, and work those stitches as instructed, making sure to pull the yarn snug when working the first stitch. Continue working in this manner, always working with only one needle at a time, working the stitches on the needle with the free end of the same needle, and leaving the other needle hanging free.

For a wide or extra-wide foot, you may want to add a few extra rows to the Foot before beginning the decreases.

The Picot Plus BO will produce a firm, nonelastic edge that will not stretch like the rest of the Slipper.

SLIPPERS
Using MC and Turkish CO, CO 74 (80) sts [37 (40) sts each needle]. Join for working in the rnd; place marker (pm) for beginning of rnd.

HEEL
Increase Rnd 1: *Needle 1:* M1-p, pm, knit to end of Needle; *Needle 2:* Knit to end of Needle, pm, M1-p—76 (82) sts [38 (41) sts each needle].
Increase Rnd 2: *Needle 1:* Purl to marker, M1-p, knit to end of Needle; *Needle 2:* Knit to marker, M1-p, purl to end—78 (84) sts.
Repeat Increase Rnd 2 once—80 (90) sts [40 (45) sts each needle].

FOOT
Work even until piece measures 2½ (2¾)" from CO edge.

SHAPE FOOT
Decrease Rnd 1: P3 (5), k22, [ME, k2tog] 10 (12) times, k22, purl to end—70 (78) sts remain [35 (39) sts each needle]. Cut yarn.

BAND

Next Rnd: Change to A. K15 (17), [yo, k2tog] 20 (22) times, knit to end.
Decrease Rnd 2: P15 (17), [p1, slip st back to left-hand needle, p2tog] 20 (22) times, purl to end—50 (56) sts remain [25 (28) sts each needle]. [Knit 1 rnd, purl 1 rnd] twice.
Bind-Off Rnd: Using Picot Plus BO, BO all sts as follows: Slip 1 wyib. *Insert tip of right-hand needle into space between second and third sts on left-hand needle and draw up a loop; place loop on left-hand needle. Slip st from right-hand needle back to left-hand needle; k2tog. Slip resulting st back to left-hand needle; k3tog. Repeat from *until 2 sts remain, 1 on each needle. Slip st from right-hand needle back to left-hand needle; k2tog. Fasten off.

THE MASTER KNITTER

"Master Knitters receive a pin and a certificate.
Since the program began in 1987, some of the knitters
are now serving on the Review Committee
for the program. Others are instructors. Others are
great knitters. All are an inspiration!"
—The Knitting Guild Association

A T THE HOME EC WORKSHOP, LISA WILCOX IS EASY TO pick out. She's the one knitting lace confidently, a pad of graph paper with careful pencil marks on it by her feet. If there's a question raised somewhere in the store, Lisa can answer it. She knows that argyle socks are knit on straight needles. She knows the best cast-off to use for a ribbed neckline. Often I have overheard her say to another knitter, "If you'd like, I can show you how."

On Saturday mornings, Lisa is part of the core group of young and old, conventional and unconventional handcrafters who meet at Home Ec's Knitter's Breakfast. With her cup of cappuccino and her slice of quiche for sustenance, she's found her knitting community. A little bit beyond middle-aged, and conservatively dressed, she jokes easily with Jason, who has long, curly hair and makes pirate dolls out of socks.

"Lisa is full of surprises," Codi, Home Ec's co-owner, once told me.

Codi's right about that. This summer, I was surprised to learn that Lisa, the seemingly quiet, unassuming knitter I had only just met, won the "Sweepstakes," an award given for garnering the most points in the knitting category at the Iowa State Fair. And what a remarkable coup that was! Lisa won blue ribbons in the following categories: Pullover Sweater (one color, fine yarn), Cardigan Sweater (two or more colors, fine yarn), Socks/Slippers (one color), Mittens/Gloves (one color), Mittens/Gloves (two or more colors), and Cap or Hat (two or more colors). Lisa also took third place in Shawl (lace) and Socks/Slippers (two or more colors), fourth place for Cap or Hat (one color), and an honorable mention for Scarf and Knitted Lace, any item.

She was still at the fair when her younger sister, Karen, had proudly announced Lisa's knitterly honors at Home Ec. Such an amazing, prodigious amount of award-winning knitting should have prepared me for the next bit of news. Still I was surprised for a second time that day when I heard that Lisa had been recently certified as a Master Knitter. The only one in Iowa.

Our little town is rich with accomplishments. Our sidewalks are etched with quotes from writers who spent time at the famous Iowa Writers' Workshop. Our local newspaper keeps us all up-to-date on the successes of the faculty and graduates at the University of Iowa. Somehow amid the buzz of new books and major grants, they missed Lisa's achievement. And so had I. Besides, being a Master Knitter was something I had thought belonged to the golden age of guilds and silk stockings knit at an impossible gauge, say seventeen stitches per inch, by young hands genetically superior to my own. I wasn't aware that there were honest-to-goodness, card-carrying Master Knitters anymore.

The concept of being a modern master, though, was very familiar to me. Almost thirty years ago, another master, intaglio printmaker

Mauricio Lasansky, had brought me to Iowa. For the four years I studied with him, I learned to make my own ink, to print consistent editions, and more important, to always push my work. Mr. Lasansky honed my critical sensibilities. Is that what it meant to be a Master Knitter? And is that why Lisa became one?

"I was looking for new goals," Lisa told me when I asked her. A knitter from age twelve, she had always found knitting pleasurable. In 2007, having raised her daughter Leah, Lisa was a new empty-nester with more free time. Hearing about The Knitting Guild Association (TKGA) Master Knitting Program in Hand Knitting, she was intrigued.

Started in 1987, The Knitting Guild Master Knitter Program is a guided independent study with three stages: advanced beginner, intermediate, and advanced. Knitting knowledge and competency is built level by level; there's no grade skipping in this school. Coursework includes not only mastering techniques, but designing patterns, writing critical reviews of books and magazines, and responding to technical questions, all reviewed by current Master Knitters. This is a rigorous curriculum, and understandably, not everyone who begins it finishes all levels. According to the guild's records, out of the 1,027 knitters ever enrolled, 787 have gone on to become Master Knitters.

But Lisa is used to demanding academic programs. Years ago, she had completed both dental school and advanced training. A practicing endodontist, she had taught in the University of Iowa's dental school for ten years. Lisa respected the Master Knitter program's clearly defined goals, focused coursework, and high standards for completion. It fit her personality, her drive, her perseverance. And so, for two years, in a creamy white Lamb's Pride Worsted, Lisa knit her way through all three levels.

Her first Level I assignment was to knit a series of four-inch by four-inch swatches on "knitting basics." Lisa thought she'd do them in a snatch. After all, they were easy: garter stitch, seed stitch, and basic cables. But after breezing through the first couple, she paused. *Her work*

was going to be judged. Lisa looked at her swatches with a more critical eye. She saw little imperfections. She noticed where improvements could be made. She knit her swatches over and over, as many as five times, before she sent them in to be evaluated. Already Lisa's critical sensibilities were being refined. All her Level I swatches, which also included a simple lace, a simple cable, and parallel increases and decreases, passed. A split stitch and uneven tension were noted, but did not require reknitting.

Moving up to Level II, Lisa advanced to paired increases and decreases, more complex cables, and lace swatches. This is when she had to knit an argyle sock, a Fair Isle mitten, and a lace doily. At this stage, every piece was evaluated by two Master Knitters. Twenty-one swatches were knit, nineteen questions researched and answered, four book reviews and a two-page historical report on knitting were written. "I had a lot of pattern revisions at this level," Lisa notes. "The committee is very thorough."

Lisa found Level III to be less frustrating than Level II. Here, she tackled the knitting summits of entrelac, brioche, mosaic, and intarsia. She designed and knit a Scandinavian sweater with at least three colors, and a hat with Aran cables and bobbles. She produced eighteen sample swatches in all. She wrote two book reviews, two magazine reviews, and two reports, one on six different knitting fibers, and the other one on Aran and Fair Isle knitting traditions. After three Master Knitters passed all her final efforts, they were re-reviewed for the last time by one of the cochairs of the Master Hand Knitting Committee.

In 2009, when Lisa Wilcox earned her Master Knitter title, she received a pin and certificate. And with that, she left behind the intuitive guesswork of knitting that sometimes leads me to drop a project or bring it to a sloppy end. She doesn't need to jiggle her stitches to make her sweaters come out nearly right. The big notebooks, the ones that contain all her work for the Master Knitter program, are now her reference. On Ravelry, she has posted photos of her course swatches, a summary of their critiques, and her own evaluations of both. She did this to aid other knitters going through the program. It's something she's sure would have helped her. Informally, online and off, Lisa does what Masters have always done—instruct.

When I finished my printmaking degree, I thought I'd never put myself through such intense study again. But brushing up against Lisa's knitting has me rethinking this. It has caused me to examine and reexamine my own knitting, analyzing how I could have done it better. Observing Lisa, I can see what it means to be a Master Knitter. It sends me back in time, to when my hands were ink-stained, when good was not enough, and when the edges of what I thought I was capable of creating softened and expanded. More than just the title, beyond the nifty pin and impressive diploma, Lisa's dedicated study has opened wide her window of knitting possibilities. Forever.

If you're at Home Ec Workshop, don't be afraid to ask Lisa how to fix the sweater sleeve you are trying to finish. The one that looks like it was tailor-made for a dolphin. Only ask her, though, if you want a straightforward, honest answer. And be prepared to reknit. Lisa has high standards. Born and raised here in Iowa City, she is our resident knitting expert, a member of the elite corps of the nation's most skilled, and those of us who have had the privilege of knowing her, laughing with her, and learning from her are very proud of our hometown Master Knitter.

For more information on the Master Knitter program, visit www.tkga.com.

LACY SCARF

DESIGNED BY THERESA GAFFEY

LIKE THE MASTER KNITTER'S PIN, KNITTING LACE OF incredible lightness and complexity is a mark of knitterly achievement. For a quick lace lesson to get you started, try this chunky scarf. A simple combination of yarnovers and purl three togethers gives this feminine pattern a beautiful richness.

....

FINISHED MEASUREMENTS
7" wide x 65" long

YARN
Lion Brand Wool-Ease Thick & Quick (80% acrylic / 20% wool; 108 yards / 170 grams): 2 skeins #134 Citron

NEEDLES
One pair straight needles size US 13 (9 mm)
Change needle size if necessary to obtain correct gauge.

NOTIONS
Stitch markers (optional)

GAUGE
9 sts and 14 rows = 4" (10 cm) in Stockinette stitch (St st)

STITCH PATTERN
BLOSSOM STITCH
(multiple before working Row 1 is 3 sts + 2; multiple before working Rows 2–4 is 5 sts + 2; 4-row repeat)
Row 1 (RS): P2, *yo, k1, yo, p2; repeat from * to end.
Row 2: K2, *p3, k2; repeat from * to end.
Row 3: P2, *k3, p2; repeat from * to end.
Row 4: K2, *p3tog, k2; repeat from * to end.
Repeat Rows 1–4 for Blossom Stitch.

SCARF
CO 14 sts. Begin Blossom Stitch; work even until piece measures 65" from the beginning, ending with Row 1 of pattern. BO all sts.

FINISHING
Block as desired.

FAE RIDGE FARM KNITTERS

*"I hope to see you all soon. Be sure and stop
out to watch the summer's magic unfold
here at the farm as the baby animals grow up and
the butterflies find a new oasis in Iowa."*
—Janette Ryan-Busch, Fae Ridge Farm newsletter

W HEN YOU FIRST MEET JANETTE RYAN-BUSCH, YOU
might find it hard to believe that she's just a little over
five feet tall. Gray-haired, bright-eyed, and slender,
Janette is a feisty bundle of energy with a huge
persona. She's passionate about everything she does. And she does a lot.

On Fae Ridge, her working farm just outside of Iowa City, Janette
grows herbs and produce. A certified organic farmer, in some places
around here, she's known as the "Basil Queen." With the aid of a llama
and an alpaca, she raises goats, sheep, chickens, rabbits, and geese. One
summer, she partnered with a local neighborhood center, bringing in a
group of at-risk kids to help with the chores and gain valuable work
experience. Janette has hosted canning workshops, fiber festivals, and
shearing days. She also spins, weaves, and knits.

Did I mention Janette has a yarn store at Fae Ridge? It's the only
one I know that also sells eggs from its own brood. Housed in a tiny
green cottage, with white shutters and a front porch, the shop looks like
it belongs in a fairy tale. Inside are shelves of the real stuff: wool and

cotton, baskets of roving. There's an ancient working cash register, and examples of Janette's work are everywhere: mittens, socks, hats, hand-dyed and hand-spun wool, toys, birdhouses made from gourds, wreaths, herbal soaps, shampoos, and more. There are pattern books, needles (wooden, of course), and all sorts of notions that have been test-driven by Janette and the group of knitters and spinners who congregate in the back, by a table stocked with goodies.

An assortment of fiber enthusiasts gather together at Fae Ridge every Saturday afternoon from eleven to five, the only time the store is open year-round (from October to January, it's also open on Sundays). The rest of the week, they may meet on the knitting social networking site Ravelry. I don't know everyone's names, because I don't get to join them that often, but I do know bits and pieces of their stories. Most important, I know what they're making.

Janette has built not only a yarn store and a place for her own handwork, but a community. On Ravelry, they define themselves as "customers and fans of Fae Ridge Farm—where knitters, spinners, felters, and dyers find socially responsible goodies for their projects and inspire, support, and guide each other through our knitting lives." That sure helps to explain why, even in the winter, when country roads can be a challenge, there's a band of the faithful congregated there.

What I love about knitting at Fae Ridge, in addition to the warm and spirited company, is knowing that in the near beyond are fields of herbs and an assembly of animals. Whenever I'm there, I feel a closeness to all things growing. Once, I arrived to find a cardboard box of baby chicks under lamps in the corner, by the baskets of roving. Another day, fiercely cold, I followed Janette to the barns to peek at her newborn goats. At Fae Ridge, Janette takes you in—to her farm, her animals, her life, and the special gang of fiber folks she's fostered. Showing up there immediately makes you a member. That's the Iowa spirit, neighborly and friendly.

When I go out to Fae Ridge, I like to wear my blue sweater, the one I knit from yarn I bought there. Thick and chunky, it's warm enough to wear as a coat on days that aren't too cold. No matter how many times I wash it, there's always a sweet barnyard smell to the wool. And when that scent starts to fade, I know it's time to grab my knitting and head back out to Fae Ridge, to soak up the goats, chickens, bunnies, and country air as well as the companionship of eccentric, strong women.

Suzanne, Robin, and Kristine are usually there when I go. A few years ago, when Suzanne and her family moved next door to Janette, she got chickens, and soon she hopes to add some milk goats. Often there are socks on Suzanne's needles and animals and children on her mind. Her daughter Lily is a friend of my youngest daughter, Lelia. Kristine and Robin are colleagues, social psychologists and professors, but at Fae Ridge, they're knitters. It's a hundred miles to Fae Ridge for Kristine, so she's been trying to grow her own local group. This spring at her university, she's teaching an honors course on knitting. Robin is an eclectic and exuberant knitter. She tells great stories as she switches between innumerable projects, which she schlepps in possibly the largest knitting bag I have ever seen.

If you happen to be in Iowa City on a Saturday, pack up your needles and wool, or stick your spinning wheel in the backseat. Don't fret if you forget your scissors or stitch markers; someone will have some to share. If you're stuck in a knitting muddle and can't figure out what you want to make next, you are headed to the right place. An opinionated cluster of knitters will inspire you. And Janette has stocked the store with everything you'll need to knit socks, sweaters—heck, anything. You might even decide you'd like to cast your lot with those who spin.

Get in your car and get going. Fae Ridge is only open a few hours a week, and you do not want to waste any time.

Take Dodge Street out of town. Go past the interstate a mile or so, turn right the moment you see Rapid Creek Road and the small Fae Ridge sign, 3.5 miles ahead.

Keep your eyes on the road. In spite of the popular notion of Iowa's flatness, Rapid Creek Road, like the rest of southeast Iowa, is all about hills and curves, so slow down.

LITTLE HEATHENS
Hard Times and High Spirits on an Iowa Farm During the Great Depression

BY MILDRED ARMSTRONG KALISH

"We take care of our own, take care of our young,
Make hay while the sun shines.
Growing our crops, singing our songs,
And planting until harvest time."
—Greg Brown, "The Iowa Waltz"

"They made their own shirts, knitted their own sweaters, scarves and socks," writes Mildred Armstrong Kalish in her tender-sweet, often hilarious, and always fascinating book, *Little Heathens*. The "they" she refers to are her maternal great-great-grandparents. "Ralph Waldo Emerson could have learned a thing or two about self-reliance from them," she continues. And there's much we can all learn from *Little Heathens*, in which we are treated to recipes, jokes, songs, home remedies, sayings, and life lessons mixed in with the stories of Mildred's rural Iowa childhood during the Great Depression. Who could ask for anything more? To quote Mildred one last time, "It was a romp."

Breathe deeply. You'll be there soon enough. Once you glimpse the little green house on your left, fenced in with chicken wire, turn in the gravel driveway and park. If you can find a space.

Don't worry about your nails, or your hair, or what you're wearing, or even what you're knitting. Leave your cares in your car. Don't bother locking it. Just walk right over and open the front door. I'll be looking for you.

GENIE'S KILLER DEVILED EGGS

When my friend Genie (see Genie's Hat, page 153) heard I was going to put a recipe for deviled eggs in this book, she said, "Use mine. They're killers. And call them Genie's Killer Deviled Eggs." A day later, she delivered a plate covered with tin foil, with a note on top: "The killers and the recipe. Make up a dozen."

12 large, hard-boiled eggs (from Fae Ridge Farm, if possible),
    cooled, peeled, and cut in half lengthwise (see Note)
2 tablespoons minced onion
⅔ cup Hellman's Real Mayonnaise
1 teaspoon Dijon mustard
1½ teaspoons curry powder
Salt and pepper, to taste
1 teaspoon paprika
Fresh parsley, for garnish

Arrange egg halves on a plate. If desired, slice the bottom of each half so that it is flat and doesn't wobble. With a teaspoon, transfer egg yolks to a small mixing bowl or the bowl of a food processor. Add onion, mayonnaise, mustard, and curry powder to yolk bowl and blend until smooth using a fork or by processing. Season with salt and pepper as desired. Spoon a scant tablespoon of egg mixture into each egg white. (Alternatively, for a fancier presentation, spoon the egg mixture into a zip-top plastic bag, close securely, then nip one of the bottom corners of the bag and squeeze the mixture into the egg white.) Sprinkle with paprika. Garnish with parsley. Serve chilled.

NOTE: My pal Anne Ylvisaker, children's book author and foodie, offers this no-fail method for hard-boiling eggs: Place eggs in a pot large enough to hold them in a single layer. Fill with enough cold water to cover the eggs by at least 1". Cover and bring water just to a boil over medium heat. Remove pot from burner and let sit for 13 to 15 minutes. Meanwhile, fill a large bowl with ice water. Remove eggs and gently submerge them in ice water (a pasta scoop works well for this). When eggs are cool enough to handle, dry and peel.

CHICKEN EGG WARMERS

ONE SATURDAY OUT AT FAE RIDGE FARM, JANETTE HANDED me a chicken egg warmer knit from an acrylic pink baby yarn with a tiny red felt bob and beak. "I got a box of these at a garage sale," she told me. They were so cute I thought I'd try to make my own version. These wool Chicken Egg Warmers will keep your soft-boiled eggs warm and cozy and will lend some playfulness to your breakfast table. Cock-a-doodle-do!

. . . .

SIZE
3" wide from beak to tail
3½" tall from edge of ribbing to top of comb

YARN
Lion Brand Lion Wool (100% wool; 158 yards / 85 grams): 1 skein each #187 Goldenrod (MC), #125 Cocoa (A), #133 Pumpkin (B), and #171 Fern (C)

NEEDLES
One set of four double-pointed needles (dpn) size US 6 (4 mm) Change needle size if necessary to obtain correct gauge.

NOTIONS
Stitch marker

GAUGE
20 sts and 32 rnds = 4" (10 cm) in Stockinette stitch (St st; knit every rnd)

STITCH PATTERNS
1x1 RIB
(multiple of 2 sts; 1-rnd repeat)
All Rnds: *K1, p1; repeat from * to end.

SEED STITCH
Rnd 1: *P1, k1; repeat from * to end.
Rnd 2: Knit the purl sts and purl the knit sts as they face you.
Repeat Rnd 2 for Seed Stitch.

BODY

Using MC, CO 26 sts. Divide sts among 3 needles [8-9-9]. Join for working in the rnd, being careful not to twist sts; place marker (pm) for beginning of rnd. Begin 1x1 Rib; work even for 1".

Next Rnd: Change to Seed st; work even until piece measures 2" from the beginning.

NECK AND HEAD

Next Rnd: BO 14 sts, k5 (including st remaining on right-hand needle), k2tog, k5—11 sts remain. Redistribute sts among 3 needles [4-3-4]. Join for working in the rnd; pm for beginning of rnd. Knit 1 rnd.

Next Rnd: *Needle 1:* Knit; *Needle 2:* K1, RLI, k1, LLI, k1; *Needle 3:* Knit—13 sts. Knit 5 rnds.

Next Rnd: *K2tog; repeat from * to last 3 sts, sk2p—6 sts remain. Cut yarn, leaving a 6" tail. Draw through remaining sts, pull tight, and fasten off.

FINISHING

Fold BO sts of Body in half. Using MC, sew half of BO sts to other half.

Tail

Using MC, wrap yarn around 1 finger 5 times. Slide loops off finger, tie knot around center of loops and sew to tail end of Body.

Beak

Using A, *work 3 Satin sts (see Special Techniques, page 158) into 1 knit st* 5 sts up from end of Body (see photo); repeat from * to * in the next knit st above the first st.

Comb

Using tapestry needle and B, make 6 loose loops through top st of Head (see photo). Cut yarn and secure to WS.

Eye

Using tapestry needle, Duplicate st (see Special Techniques, page 158), and C, work Eyes 6 rows up from end of Seed st and 2 rows in from beak on each side of Head.

A QUICKENING OF
THE HEART

"And none will hear the postman's knock
Without a quickening of the heart,
For who can bear to feel himself forgotten?"
—W. H. Auden, "Night Mail"

O NCE, SEVERAL YEARS AGO, DESPERATE FOR THE COMPANY of other knitters, I spotted a tiny hand-knit sock hanging proudly over the rearview mirror in the car parked next to mine, and I left a note under the car's windshield wiper. Written on a sock yarn's ball band, it included my phone number and e-mail address.

My three daughters, who were with me at the time, were horrified. "She'll think you're a stalker," my middle daughter, Flory, warned me.

But she was wrong. My ball band note got me an invitation to a knitting group.

These days, it's hard to imagine being such a desperate knitter. There are blogs, knitalongs, and the knitting social networking site

Ravelry. In my small town, we now have several fine yarn stores with sociable knitters sitting around, click-clacking away, most of them eager to chat. What's more, not long after I left that note, I started writing knitting stories for the Lion Brand Yarn Company's online newsletter, and a wonderful thing happened. Friendly e-mails arrived from readers—knitters. Over time, an amazing group has reached out and checked in. And when they do, in camaraderie, they often tell their own stories.

Stories about socks, for example. Socks knit in khaki to be sent to uncles and fathers, soldiers during World War II—all returned safely, I was assured. Socks also knit for soldiers in World War I, this time stitched by a grandfather who, riding on trains for business, used this time to "knit his bit." Socks knit for boyfriends who later became husbands, and those who didn't. Socks knit in patterns featuring a cigarette with clouds of angora smoke. Socks knit in the darkness of movie theaters.

Knitters have written me stories about what was knit for them. Sweaters too tight. Too itchy. Just perfect. Purple. They have told me stories of what they knit for others. And knowing about the children's books I've written, they've told me about their own favorite children's books. Like *Strawberry Girl* by Lois Lenski and *Miss Rumphius* by Barbara Cooney. Favorites of mine, too.

In tender, touching e-mails, knitters have reflected modestly about their own generosity—their acts of compassion. Like giving away the mittens off their own hands or knitting hats with matching dog sweaters for the homeless and their pets. They've knit slippers to warm the feet of an entire school while they took their standardized tests, and mittens to be put in food baskets. Those are just a few of the many stories from the knitting fortress out there, and hearing them—making the acquaintance of these knitters—inspires me. It gives me great hope. And any time I write about charitable knitting needs, a new bumper crop of the big-hearted respond almost immediately: *Count me in.*

Knitters treat me to stories about where they knit, like on the back of a husband's motorcycle, as Elizabeth Zimmermann did. (Not great for lace knitting, I'm advised, so better to take along a dishcloth, or maybe a scarf.) They knit in church, where I am guessing you can knit whatever you'd like. Likewise for knitting in a courtroom, at bingo, at the racetrack, or in Norway—near the top of globe, when the snow's finally melting.

Knitters trade tales of their mothers, grandmothers, grandfathers, aunts, uncles, sisters, and brothers who knit. They tell me of the sisterhood of their knitting teachers, including neighbors and strangers. They tell me about their childhoods in Canada, on Coney Island, in England, and on gravel roads not far from where I live. Generously, knitters have answered my questions about those childhoods, research for future children's books I hope someday to write. Crossing state lines, international borders, the expansive vistas of generations and beliefs, these knitters and their stories are proof that what's on our needles tells its own tale.

Knitters have sent me birthday wishes, congratulations, greetings, sympathies. Many have paused to tell me about their own joys and sorrows, hardships, heartaches, and triumphs. They have asked for knitting advice and crochet patterns.

Thank you for writing. That's the way I usually start my response to readers' e-mails. But that's not enough. Not big enough. Not warm enough. Not soft enough for the richness they have given me. The arrival of their e-mails quickens my heart. Their stories have given me the courage and confidence to go on telling mine. Their kind words, their caring messages, have made me feel wanted, connected, and so far away from that tiny sign of community knitting in a random parking lot.

CHAPTER 4

Legacy

YARN BEGAN IT ALL

"We will always be blessed by the ties
that bind and that yarn that began it all."
—Rainbow Socks cofounder
Babbie Cameron, June 2009

AINBOW SOCKS. MORE LIKE SLIPPERS. MY BLUE, GOLD, red, cream, and deep turquoise ones are in great condition, never worn. Finely knit, eight stitches to an inch, they look small, almost child-sized. I hadn't imagined they might fit me, but just yesterday, after all these years, I discovered that they do. I'll keep them on until this story's written. After all, along with the yarn and the knitters who made them, they are characters in this tale. And besides, my feet are always cold, even on this summer day.

I was searching for signs of goodness in the universe when I stumbled on the Knitting Project. It was 1994. Winter. The war in the former Yugoslavia had created thousands of refugees, mostly women and children. Many of them were knitters, who had left yarn and tools behind along with their former lives. Hands idle, they were spending their days in cold, uncomfortable limbos. Some had even started to pull apart their own sweaters, aching for wool and using whatever they could find to knit—a bicycle spoke as a knitting needle, for instance. Aid workers and mental health therapists helping them with post-traumatic stress disorder sent out a call: Would it be possible to get these women needles and yarn?

From that heartrending request, from that cry from across the Atlantic, the Knitting Project began. In a span of almost seven years, it sent more than thirty-two tons of yarn and needles. Donations came from knitters in every state of the Union, and from several American mills where workers volunteered their Saturdays to make the yarn.

"A mountain of yarn," is how Babbie Cameron, the Knitting Project cofounder, once described the contribution they received. A mountain of yarn that put knitting back into anxious, troubled hands. Visiting the refugee knitters after an early yarn shipment, Babbie and her husband, Stu, were presented with a pair of *sarene carape*, traditional Balkan slippers. Knit with the donated yarn, they were the first Rainbow Socks. Taking a duffel bag of them back to the States, the Camerons promised to sell as many as they could. And for the next six years, they did. Filling her house, devoting herself to the women who needed her, Babbie launched her nonprofit, Rainbow Socks. The socks, and later, mittens and kilim rugs, were sold through church groups, humanitarian organizations, knitting guilds, and ads in knitting magazines. Maybe you even own a pair. I bought dozens.

"When you look inside your rainbows, you will find the signature of a refugee knitter, and you will be holding in your hand a connection that links you to her future," stated the Rainbow Socks order form. Indeed, the sock money that hundreds of women earned was used for firewood, eyeglasses, shoes, blood pressure medication, and fresh fruit for their children.

After sending my first yarn shipment in 1994, I designed cards for the Knitting Project and many of its offspring efforts. The cards were used for thank-yous and sold in packs as fund-raisers. For my tiny contribution to this monumental work helping refugee women and their children, I was rewarded a hundredfold with a knit baby sweater, other small pieces of handwork, touching notes from the women translated by volunteers, newsletters with updates on the women whose names I was learning as time went on, and stories of their trials and progress, concerns and worries. Later, when I met Babbie and Stu, I received a large mounted photo of a Rainbow Sock knitter that has a permanent place in my studio. The Knitting Project—Rainbow Socks, along with its later related ventures—continued until the winter of 2000, but all that it created by giving, by helping other knitters to survive through terrible, trying times, has willed me a lifetime supply of the goodness I had been searching for back then.

Our Rainbow Socks were well worn and loved by me and my children. The ones on my feet now are the very last ones I have. I was saving them. But this pair fits me so perfectly, I think it's time to use them. After all, they were meant for wear. And their story is almost told. To end it, I'll honor their legacy with this bit of unsolicited advice: Make room in your knitting life for others. Share the warmth.

KNITTING FOR PEACE
Make the World a Better Place
One Stitch at a Time

BY BETTY CHRISTIANSEN

"We knitters work a powerful magic when we knit for others.
By doing so, as you will see in the pages that follow, we can build bridges
between warring nations, help to heal deep wounds, offer a
primal sort of comfort, and create peace—however small, and in
whatever way may be—for others and ourselves."
—Betty Christiansen, *Knitting for Peace*

Betty Christiansen knows and understands the legacy of charitable knitting. And in her beautifully designed book, *Knitting for Peace*, she shares her passion for the subject. Taking us around the globe, Christiansen introduces us to wartime knitters, political knitters, refugee knitters, prison knitters, and spiritual knitters, young and old, all stitching for the needy. There are inspirational interviews with folks like Evie Rosen, who started Warm Up America! to provide blankets to the homeless, and Peter Haggerty, whose fears of another war led him to found a most hopeful business, Peace Fleece, as well as with many lesser-known individuals and groups involved in meaningful initiatives. Along with their inspiring stories and guidelines for getting involved in their efforts, there are fifteen patterns suitable for charitable giving: hats, shawls, mittens, socks, vests, sweaters, and more.

Knitting for Peace is an historical reference, a spiritual guide, a charitable knitting handbook, and a great read. Once it is on your bookshelf, you will find yourself reaching for it again and again.

LATKES

Potatoes, grated, baked, fried, boiled, even raw, have sustained hearts, souls, and bodies through the most difficult of times. Potato pancakes, or latkes, are common in Central and Eastern European cuisines, and are traditionally served at Hanukkah throughout the world. If desired, you can fry and bake the latkes up to an hour in advance.

2 large eggs
2 medium-sized yellow onions
8 medium russet potatoes, washed, peeled, and dried (see Note)
¼ cup matzo meal or crushed saltines
Salt, to taste
¼–½ cup vegetable oil, for frying
Sour cream, jam, applesauce, or salsa, for topping

Place a large cast-iron or heavy frying pan over medium-high heat, Place a cookie sheet in oven and preheat to 325°F.

In a small bowl, beat the eggs.

Peel the onions and cut them into pieces large enough to grate or small enough for the food processor grater. Grate the potatoes and onions either by hand or in the food processor, as follows: potato, onion, potato, onion. If there is a lot of liquid when you are done, transfer mixture to a strainer and press it out.

Transfer potato mixture to a large bowl. Add beaten egg and enough matzo meal to make the batter stick together lightly.

Put oil in a measuring cup and, using a silicone or pastry brush, coat the hot pan. Make sure you generously cover the entire surface. Plop a tablespoon of the batter into the pan. If it sizzles, oil is ready. Lower burner temperature at any point if oil begins smoking.

Drop the potato mixture in ¼-cup clumps into the oil. Very lightly brown latkes for about 1 or 2 minutes on each side. Move them to a plate and gently blot with a paper towel. Transfer blotted latkes to the cookie sheet in oven. Latkes in oven will continue to cook and brown while you fry the rest. Reapply oil to pan and continue frying latkes until batter is used up. Latkes in oven are ready when brown and crisp.

Serve hot with an assortment of toppings.

Makes twenty-four 3" to 4" latkes; serves about 6.

NOTE: Once you have peeled the potatoes, you need to make the latkes quickly; peeled potatoes turn an ugly green if they are left out too long.

MITTEN LADIES

*"People will never remember me for what I have in life.
They'll remember me for what I've given others."*
—Marge Snyder, Mitten Lady of Janesville, Wisconsin
As told to Marv Wopat, *The Janesville Gazette*,
December 21, 2008, on why she kept knitting mittens even
after her hand was paralyzed by a stroke.

O N BENCHES AT HIGH SCHOOL FOOTBALL GAMES, ON THE hard plastic seating of hospital waiting rooms, on plump living-room sofas, on straight-backed wooden chairs by kitchen tables with coffee and companions, wherever they can set up shop, the ladies are at work. Hard times and economic woes don't affect their labor for others. They only deepen it.

Some are known for what they do. Others wish to remain unrecognized and unheralded, revealing themselves only to family and friends. They arrange to have their efforts picked up at their front door, quickly drop off plastic bags bulging with goods, or leave their neat bundles for others to use to decorate a giving tree.

Who are these women?

Why, they're the Mitten Ladies. Volunteers in the service of protecting vulnerable hands, they stock our communities and world with their knitted and crocheted mittens. I'll bet there's one in your town. Maybe even two or three.

The year I decided to change my karma by knitting one hundred mittens, I almost became one myself. But when my last pair of mittens was finished, I moved on to other projects, something true Mitten Ladies never do. A story idea, one about an old lady who knits mittens, led me to play with the moniker. For fun, I Googled it. What popped up amazed me. Obituaries and feature articles about Mitten Ladies from newspapers all over the country: Helen Solka, Audrey Thompson, Marjorie Schulz, Elsie E. Howe, Dorothy Louise (Scott) Grant Tanguay, Anna Duell, Anne Buly, Patricia "Pat" Bangs, Ruth Haley, Lela Mills, Marge Snyder, Terri Crossman, Helen Bunce.

Helen Bunce's *New York Times* obituary was written by the celebrated obit writer Robert G. Thomas Jr. Widely read, often reproduced and included in anthologies, it's appropriately titled "The Mitten Lady." Helen was an anonymous contributor to local and worldwide efforts, and her identity was disclosed only days before her death, after forty-seven years and more than four thousand mittens.

Let's pause here a moment for some mitten talk, for the clarification needed to understand the magnitude of these stitching efforts. "One hundred mittens" really means one hundred pairs—two hundred mittens. It's the sheer numbers that make these knitters Mitten Ladies, and many of them do keep count: fifty mittens in 1955, one hundred mittens in 1978, four thousand mittens in a lifetime.

There's usually a story behind their devotion, one that gets better with each pair of mittens, because after a while, knitting the mittens becomes the story. Helen Bunce's tale began with a sermon she had heard. In the ruins of post–World War II Europe, there stood a cold little boy. Waiting in a relief line for some warm mittens, he left without getting any. When his turn had come, there were none left. "Need is unending" was the message. That's why Helen and other Mitten Ladies knit on and on: so there might be enough for all the children. Even the ones at the very end of a very long line.

Mitten Ladies raise families, work jobs, take care of ailing relatives, suffer their own losses and hardships, battle their own demons. And through it all, they faithfully knit volumes of warmth for those in need. They deserve a place in women's history. It's not just mittens that they give, it's what their dedication teaches us about living, about being a citizen of the world, about accepting that even modest means are a privilege, and then, about using that privilege to work for the greater good.

Mittens are easily mastered. Knit on two, four, or five needles, they can be plain Janes: one color, stockinette stitch. Stripes are simple to add. If you want to be a Mitten Lady, you will need a good pattern and a sturdy knitting bag with a pocket for notions. Oh, and you might just want to slip in a small notebook to jot down changes or innovations to what will become your mitten pattern. A section in the back can be devoted exclusively to keeping track: ten pairs in 2009, twenty in 2010, and so on.

If you do decide to be a Mitten Lady, you may want to take your knitting everywhere you go, knit every chance you have. You'll soon figure out the best thumbs. You'll learn that markers can be replaced by a purl stitch and that left and right mittens can be made interchangeable. Knitting a dozen pairs could make you an expert.

Snow is falling as I write this. It's perfect weather for sledding or building a snowman. But not without mittens. Somewhere, right now, there's a lady at work, ribbing a cuff, increasing for a thumb gusset, knitting a child some winter warmth. It could be you.

THE ENDLESS STEPPE

BY ESTHER HAUTZIG

The Mitten Ladies create warmth for the cold hands of those unable to knit for themselves. What happens when the knitter is the one in need? In *The Endless Steppe*, Esther Hautzig's autobiographical novel about her childhood in Siberia, we are afforded a rare and touching account of a heroic and spunky twelve-year-old girl who uses her knitting to earn food for her destitute, starving family. Her uncrushable spirit is tested along the way. Facing challenges that would have broken most knitters' resolve, Esther Hautzig knits on with courage, confidence, and bravery, and so, like the Mitten Ladies, she inspires us to do the same. Read *The Endless Steppe*, and you'll be grateful for the power vested in our needles.

MITTEN LADIES
SLOW-COOKER SOUP

While this thick soup cooks in a slow cooker, you can stitch a pair of easy mittens.

1 medium onion, diced
2 cups mushrooms, sliced
3 large garlic cloves, minced
2 stalks celery with leaves, thinly sliced
3 medium carrots, cut into ½" chunks
3 medium potatoes, cut into eighths
2 dried bay leaves
2 cups yellow split peas, rinsed
8 cups chicken broth
1 (20-ounce) package lean turkey bratwurst

Preheat oven to 350°F. Heat a 13"-by-18" baking pan.

Turn a 6- to 8-quart slow cooker to high. Add all ingredients in order listed. Cover and put a weight on top of lid to keep heat and steam from escaping. Cook 5 to 5½ hours, until yellow peas are soft or dissolved; if soup is too thick, thin with a little extra chicken broth. Remove sausages. Cut them into ½" pieces and put back into soup. Stir well and serve.

Serves 8.

QUICK AND EASY MITTENS
(AKA PEARL)

IN HONOR OF MITTEN LADIES, PAST, PRESENT, AND FUTURE, I introduce these Quick and Easy Mittens, perfect for your own family's needs and charitable donations. I've nicknamed this pattern Pearl because there is a purl stitch serving as a stitch marker on either side of the thumb gusset. Pearl is a sister pattern to the Quick and Easy Socks on page 73 because, until you put the thumb stitches on a holder, you can still change your mind and make socks instead.

. . . .

SIZE

X-Small (Small, Medium, Large, X-Large)
To fit 3–6 years, (6–8 years, Adult Small/Medium, Adult Large, Adult X-Large)

NOTE: *For denser, super-warm Mittens, work the pattern 1 size larger than needed and felt the Mittens lightly in the washing machine, checking every 2 or 3 minutes until the Mittens are the size you want. Make sure not to leave them in too long, since there's no going back once they're felted. If you prefer your Mittens to be machine washable, you may substitute Lion Brand Yarn Wool-Ease Chunky (153 yards / 140 grams), but remember that machine-washable yarn cannot be felted.*

FINISHED MEASUREMENTS

5½ (6½, 7½, 8½, 9½)" circumference
7 (7¾, 10, 10¾, 11½)" long

YARN

Lion Brand Alpine Wool (100% wool; 93 yards / 85 grams): 1 (1, 1, 2, 2) skein(s) #123 Bay Leaf

One set of five double pointed needles (dpn) size US 6 (4 mm)
One set of five double pointed needles size US 8 (5 mm)
Change needle size if necessary to obtain correct gauge.

NOTIONS
Stitch holder

GAUGE
15 sts and 20 rnds = 4" (10 cm) in Stockinette stitch (St st; knit every rnd),
using larger needles

STITCH PATTERN
1x1 RIB
(multiple of 2 sts; 1-rnd repeat)

MITTENS (both alike)
CUFF
Using smaller needles and Long-Tail CO (see Special Techniques,
page 158), CO 20 (24, 28, 32, 36) sts. Divide sts among 4 needles [5-5-5-5
(6-6-6-6, 7-7-7-7, 8-8-8-8, 9-9-9-9)]. Begin 1x1 Rib; work even for 12 (13, 15,
16, 18) rnds.

HAND
Next Rnd: Change to St st (knit every rnd); work even for 3 rnds.

SHAPE THUMB
NOTE: The purl sts on Needles 1 and 2 mark where you will work the
increases on each Increase Rnd. You will work the increase on Needle
1 after the purl st, and the increase on Needle 2 before the purl st. If
you prefer, you may omit placing the markers and use the purl sts as
your markers.
Increase Rnd 1: *Needle 1:* K4 (5, 6, 7, 8), pm (optional), p1, LLI; *Needle 2:*
RLI, pm (optional), p1, k4 (5, 6, 7, 8); *Needles 3 and 4:* Knit—22 (26, 30, 34,
38) sts [6-6-5-5 (7-7-6-6, 8-8-7-7, 9-9-8-8, 10-10-9-9)]. Work even for 2 rnds.

Increase Rnd 2: Increase 2 sts this rnd, then every 3 rnds 2 (3, 3, 4, 4) times, as follows: *Needle 1:* Knit to marker (or to purl st if you didn't place a marker), slip marker (sm), p1, RLI, knit to end of needle; *Needle 2:* Knit to marker (or to purl st), LLI, sm, p1, knit to end of needle; *Needles 3 and 4:* Knit—28 (34, 38, 44, 48) sts [9-9-5-5 (11-11-6-6, 12-12-7-7, 14-14-8-8, 15-15-9-9)].

Next Rnd: K5 (6, 7, 8, 9), place next 8 (10, 10, 12, 12) sts on holder for Thumb, removing markers if you placed them, knit to end—20 (24, 28, 32, 36) sts remain [5-5-5-5 (6-6-6-6, 7-7-7-7, 8-8-8-8, 9-9-9-9)].

Work even until piece measures 6 (6¼, 8¼, 8½, 9)" from the beginning, or to 1 (1½, 1¾, 2¼, 2½)" less than desired length.

NOTE: For the correct Mitten length, Mitten should reach the top of the little finger before beginning shaping.

MITTEN TOP

Decrease Rnd: Decrease 4 sts this rnd, then every other rnd 2 (3, 4, 5, 6) times, as follows: *Needles 1–4:* *Knit to last 2 sts on needle, k2tog—8 sts remain (2-2-2-2). Cut yarn, leaving 5" tail. Thread tail through remaining sts, pull tight, and fasten off.

THUMB

Transfer sts from waste yarn to 3 larger needles, being careful not to twist sts—8 (10, 10, 12, 12) sts. Rejoin yarn. Join for working in the rnd; pm for beginning of rnd. Begin St st; work even until Thumb measures 1 (1¼, 1½, 2, 2)" from end of shaping.

Decrease Rnd: *K2tog; repeat from * to end—4 (5, 5, 6, 6) sts remain. Cut yarn, leaving 5" tail. Thread tail through remaining sts, pull tight, and fasten off.

FINISHING

Sew gaps at Thumb.

GOLDEN HANDS

"And what is a stitch for? To hold.
It binds past to present, old century to
new, generation to generation."
—Veronica Patterson, *PieceWork* magazine,
November/December 1993

WHEN I WAS GROWING UP IN THE 1960S, EVERY Memorial Day carfuls of Epsteins gathered for a family reunion. The hosts, my father's first cousins, had a hobby farm in New Jersey—a rural paradise complete with a pond for swimming, or, if you were so inclined, for paddling about in their wooden rowboat. Throughout the day, across the open spaces of the farm, I would stumble into gatherings of relatives engaged in lively, intelligent conversations, arguments, and discussions, both personal and political. The farm is where I first tasted lasagna, first saw a room-sized loom, and first came to understand that large chunks of my personality, both good and bad, were directly linked to this assembly of loud and opinionated people.

The Epstein family reunions are history. My father died in 1975, and since then, death and old age has claimed most of his generation. This is a story about an afghan that gave me one piece of my family back.

My father believed his sister, my aunt Florence, had the Epsteins' "golden hands," like our cousins on the farm who wove, made their own winter coats, and once explained to a much younger, much less knowledgeable me, the concept of steeks. My father thought his sister could make anything. He loved telling about Aunt Florence and her friend Leah, whom we all called Aunt Leah, and the business they created, sewing gowns and other fancy clothes. Two sets of golden hands working side by side.

"Mom did the hems," my cousin Gerri told me recently. "And the beading, too. She hand-beaded wedding gowns like mine."

I remember those gowns. They were beautiful.

"It was Aunt Leah who sewed and cut. She was the talent," Gerri continued.

But not in my father's stories. Even during their frequent and bitter arguments, he spoke proudly of his sister's extraordinary talents. Their difficult and stormy relationship is one of the many reasons I never really knew my aunt outside of the tales my father told. But that's another story. My cousins and I have elected to leave our parents' battles behind, and become friends.

"You know, my mother loved to crochet and knit, too," my cousin Gerri told me after reading one of my early knitting essays. "It gave her great pleasure."

Remembering only the beaded wedding gowns, I had almost forgotten that my aunt with the golden hands had also knit and crocheted. I had almost forgotten the awe-inspiring white beret with loops and sequins she made me when I was about twelve. And it had never before occurred to me that Aunt Florence might have known the same joys that I experience when knitting.

"Would you like one of Mom's afghans?" Gerri asked a few months later when I was visiting her.

Would I? For years, I have been buying hand-knit samplers, mittens, booties, socks, and shawls abandoned by other people's families from vintage and resale shops. Even though they weren't made for me, these orphaned knits give me a sense of the family history and tradition I long for and miss. Now my cousin was offering me something I never dreamed I would receive at this point in my life, one of my own family's treasures.

"Brights, darks, or rainbow colors?" she asked.

Packed away, deep in her attic, she explained, were boxes of her mother's afghans, organized by color. Taking my order for brights, she promised that after my visit, she'd unearth one and send it to me.

A few weeks later, it arrived. Lifting it out of the cardboard mailing box, I could feel the weight of what must have been a couple pounds of yarn. Crocheted in a ripple pattern, with a wide shell stitch border, it was generous in size and color, worked in a palette only possible with synthetic dyes and fiber. A vintage piece in perfect condition, made by my very own aunt with her golden hands.

For several years, Aunt Florence's afghan has made the rounds of our rooms, its presence always homey and comforting. On the small sofa by the TV in the room outside my studio, my middle daughter, Flory, and I huddled with it while we waited out a devastating tornado that hit our town a few years ago. Lately it's been in the living room, where I read, knit, and think. Draped over the couch across from my chair, it seems to be inviting me to relax a bit, to put my knitting down, to stop doing chores, and to snuggle under its colors and warmth. To rest awhile.

I've had plenty of opportunity to study Aunt Florence's afghan. Evident in this large, vibrant canvas is the enjoyment my aunt had in playing with the colors, the risks she took adding a row of orange after rows of light purple and pale pink, or a bright red after a sky blue, and the delight she must have felt watching how those unlikely couplings could create such a beautiful color scene. There have been times when I have carried back her adventurousness to my own knitting. Connecting across stitches and patterns, I now understand something about my aunt through what we both share.

"She made lots and lots of baby sweaters and hats and afghans. Always without instructions, always for others," Gerri told me. "She never even used a blanket herself. She just enjoyed making them and giving them away. She made them for us and the kids, and her afghans were raffled off at charitable events and fund-raisers, and donated to those who were in need."

Without instructions, my cousin also repeated several times. Unlike my mother, or my aunt Charlotte, or many other knitters I have met, Aunt Florence never needed to look down at her work or pay close attention to what her fingers were doing. She was able to do this because she chose simple patterns, like the ripple one, easily memorized and full of repetition. Her established hand-mind connection freed her to move quickly through skein after skein. I can and often do work that way.

"Always for others" is how my cousin described her mother's making and giving. Embedded in that is the satisfying sense of contributing in a tiny way to helping those in need. It's what has driven me to knit piles of preemie hats, bundles of washcloths, and bags of Warm Up America! squares. When I knitted and donated a hundred pairs of mittens, my children rolled their eyes and nicknamed me the mitten factory. They don't understand why I do this. Yet. But I now know my aunt Florence would. I am following a family tradition—hers.

Here's how an afghan is more than an afghan. Receiving Aunt Florence's afghan was a reunion, like the reunions on the farm when all the Epsteins congregated and my roots were on display. And attending this reunion by looking for the clues led me to find my own Aunt Florence story. This one. Not magical like my father's golden hands stories, but just as special.

UPDATED RIPPLE AFGHAN

DESIGNED BY THERESA GAFFEY

T HIS IS AN UPDATED, KNITTED VERSION OF THE CLASSIC ripple stitch afghan pattern my aunt Florence loved. Knit one for your family. And if you get into the ripple knitting groove, like Aunt Florence did, keep on going. Send your rippled warmth out into the world to folks at nursing homes, hospitals, hospice centers, homeless shelters, schools, and daycare centers.

- -

FINISHED MEASUREMENTS
45" wide x 54" long

YARN
Lion Brand Vanna's Choice (100% premium acrylic; 170 yards / 100 grams): 3 skeins each #110 Navy (A), #099 Linen (C), and #170 Pea Green (E); 2 balls #149 Silver Grey (D); 1 ball #173 Dusty Green (B)

NEEDLES
One 29" long or longer circular (circ) needle size US 10 (6 mm) needles
Change needle size if necessary to obtain correct gauge.

GAUGE
14 sts and 28 rows = 4" (10 cm) in Garter stitch (knit every row)

GARTER ZIGZAG

(multiple of 30 sts + 3; 2-row repeat)

NOTE: Work CO sts within the pattern using Backward Loop CO (see Special Techniques, page 158).

Row 1 (RS): K1, skp, *k13, CO 1 st, k1, CO 1 st, k13, s2kp2; repeat from * to last 30 sts, k13, CO 1 st, k1, CO 1 st, k13, k2tog, k1.

Row 2: K1, p1, *k14, p1; repeat from * to last st, k1.

Repeat Rows 1 and 2 for Garter Zigzag.

STRIPE SEQUENCE

*Working in Garter Zigzag, work 20 rows (10 Garter ridges) in A, 4 rows (2 ridges) in B, 16 rows (8 ridges) in C, 8 rows (4 ridges) in D, then 20 rows (10 ridges) in E; repeat from * for Stripe Sequence.

AFGHAN

Using A, CO 213 sts. Begin Garter Zigzag; work even until piece measures approximately 54" from the beginning, ending with next-to-last row of Stripe Sequence. Continuing with E, BO all sts knitwise.

FINISHING

Block as desired.

IOWA KNITTER

*"Do not start another pair of gloves with
leftover yarn. Please return all unused yarn to Chapter."*
—The American Red Cross,
Gloves (for Servicemen) pattern, January 1942

OOPED UP IN OUR COOL HOUSE ONE HOT AND VERY HUMID summer day, my kids decided we should brave the heat and break up our boredom by going to Artifacts, a vintage resale store worthy of its name. So we piled into the car and cranked up the air conditioning. When we got there, the kids rushed straight to the clothing department in the back. I lingered in the front, browsing through shelves cluttered with what could have been the artifacts of my childhood—toys, jewelry, fabric, and dishes from the sixties.

I hadn't been there long when I noticed the socks over by the humming air conditioner. Big and red with gray and tan toes, they looked like the socks the woodsman in "Little Red Riding Hood" would wear. Who really wore them? I wondered. And who knit them? They were sturdy socks knit from the toe up, something like a Balkan slipper sock. A foreign way of making socks, I thought. They were knit confidently from scrap yarn, perhaps what remained from hats and mittens the knitter had made for her woodsman husband and elf children. There was a shawl, too: lavender, light and lofty, knit from Shetland wool with an even and steady gauge. The moth holes seemed to dance on the perfect knit and purl stitches.

I brought both items to the counter and asked Todd, the owner, where they had come from.

"I got them at an estate sale," he told me.

Did he know the socks were knit toe up? Did he know this was a clue to where the knitter came from? My children, my best social critics, were too busy trying on clothes to stop me from chattering on about my fascination.

Todd listened patiently and then said, "There were needles, too. Bone, I think. Would you be interested?"

"Yes, always," I told Todd. And I thought about how lucky I was. I would soon have some piece of local knitting history. I'm not sure why wool and needles, shawls and socks, and a knitter I never knew meant so much to me on that sweltering summer day, but I was touched by the connection all the same, and I speculated loftily whether there might be a message for me in this knitter's legacy.

Todd told me the needles were buried within boxes of other treasures he had purchased that day. He promised me that as soon as he had unpacked them, he would let me know. Meantime, I had the socks and shawl to appreciate during the long, hot summer ahead of me with three kids home from school.

Months later, when summer was over, Todd ran into my husband, Rody, at our food co-op. "Tell Michelle I have the knitting stuff she wanted," he said. "Have her drop by anytime."

The very next day, I made it to the store. Behind the counter a thin, narrow box decorated with delicate flowers was waiting for me. Inside were hand-carved bone knitting needles and crocket hooks, a cardboard package of six size-1 nickel-plated knitting needles, and, folded crisply and tucked under the cardboard package, a World War II Red Cross pattern leaflet, with instructions for knitting gloves for our servicemen.

The pattern discovery helped me place this Iowa knitter in time and gave me a clue to her intent. But did it reveal anything else? The pattern looked barely used. Was that because she had memorized it? Or did bad news—a loved one killed in the war—cause her to put away her needles and the pattern? Could she have dutifully stored them for the next knitter, for the next war, because her war was finally over and her beloveds would soon return?

It was a cold autumn day, the maple leaves bright and fluttering and the prairie wind fierce. Perfect knitting weather. I took my rectangular box of treasures home. I laid all the contents out on the table near my own knitting. I went upstairs and found those huge woodsman socks. They were not so huge when I tried them on. I went back downstairs and wrapped myself in the lavender shawl.

The house was quiet, and the kids were at school. I should have been working on my new book. But I couldn't head down to my studio, to my private little inner world, just yet. Right now, I was enveloped in this other world. The world of this box and these hand-carved needles and the official Red Cross pattern for war-weary hands.

I made some hot tea and poured it into a cup that had belonged to my mother. I sat down in my knitting chair, my tea resting on its arm, my new needles and hooks, from an unknown Iowa knitter, in my lap. The wind was howling outside. The sky was heavy and gray. Maybe it would snow that night. Or the next day. Soon, surely.

I tried out the carved bone crochet hook first. I had never seen or used bone before. I took some of my leftover sock yarn and crocheted some simple patches. A small tool, with an ornate top, it warmed as I worked with it. I tested the nickel-plated needles, too, knitting more squares. I could use all of them for an afghan. My oldest would be going away to college in a year, and it would be grand to make her something enduring like a fine-gauge patchwork cover, something that might last longer than my lifetime. Did the Iowa knitter, whose needles I was now using, make her lavender shawl and woodsman socks wishing them to be around for the generations to come?

I worked another patch and drank my tea. Branches scraped against the side of the house. The wind was picking up force. I was glad to be inside, knitting peacefully, thoughtfully. In another room, in our cedar chest, were hand-knit baby blankets, little sweaters, hats, and mittens I had made. When I'm no longer around, I wondered, would my children—or grandchildren—feel the burden of too many things, the clutter of their past, and unload them somewhere too?

One day, after my needles are put away for good, will a harried mother on a hot summer day, with a small flock of bored kids in tow, reach across a counter somewhere to touch the blanket I made for my firstborn? Will she delight, as I did, to find it along with a cache of knitter's tools, and perhaps, a creased World War II Red Cross pattern for servicemen's gloves? And will she, while tending to scraped knees and hurt feelings, while fixing dinners and reading bedtime stories, pause and try to imagine the knitter who left them behind? After we are gone, does our knitting outlive us by forging new bonds with kindred souls?

The Iowa knitter's pattern and her box of tools now belong to me. Someday, with her needles, I might make a pair of those Red Cross gloves for servicemen. And knowing that these needles and hooks might someday find themselves in the hands of yet another knitter, I might even neatly write in the margins a few tips for that next knitter, adding to what was passed on to me. Then, using the decades-old crease as my guide, I'll refold the pattern, put the needles back in their cardboard sleeve, and close the box.

VICTORY SCARF
AND WRISTERS

T HIS SCARF AND MITTEN SET, KNIT IN SOFT AND BEAUTIFUL Amazing yarn, is loaded with victory Vs. Knit it for friends and loved ones. Make extras to donate to those engaged in struggles and strife. May they be worn in peace and good health.

. . . .

FINISHED MEASUREMENTS

Scarf: 6¾" wide x 54" long, slightly stretched
Wristers: Approximately 6" hand circumference
NOTE: Wristers will stretch to fit nearly any size hand.

YARN

Lion Brand Yarn Amazing (53% wool / 47% acrylic: 147 yards / 50 grams): 2 skeins #202 Rainforest
NOTE: Two skeins will make both the Scarf and Wristers.

NEEDLES

Scarf: One pair straight needles size US 6 (4 mm)
Wristers: One set of five double-pointed needles (dpn) size US 4 (3.5 mm)
Change needle size if necessary to obtain correct gauge.

NOTIONS

Wristers: Stitch marker, stitch holder

GAUGE

Scarf: 16 sts and 22 rows = 4" (10 cm) in Stockinette stitch (St st)
Wristers: 18 sts and 26 rows = 4" (10 cm) in Stockinette stitch

4X1 RIB
(multiple of 5 sts + 7; 1-row repeat)
Row 1 (WS): K1, p2, *k1, p4; repeat from * to last 3 sts, k1, p2, k1.
Row 2: Knit the knit sts and purl the purl sts as they face you.
Repeat Row 2 for 4x1 Rib.

SCARF V PATTERN
(multiple of 5 sts + 7; 4-row repeat)
Set-Up Rows 1 (RS) and 3: Knit.
Set-Up Rows 2 and 4: K1, purl to last st, k1.
Row 5: K3, *p1, k4; repeat from * to last 4 sts, p1, k3.
Row 6: K1, p1, *k1, p1, k1, p2; repeat from * to last 5 sts, [k1, p1] twice, k1.
Row 7: Repeat Row 1.
Row 8: Repeat Row 2.
Repeat Rows 5-8 for Scarf V Pattern.

WRISTERS V PATTERN
(multiple of 5 sts + 5; 4-rnd repeat)
Rnds 1 and 2: Knit.
Row 3: K2, *p1, k4; repeat from * to last 3 sts, p1, k2.
Row 4: K2, p1, k1, *p2, k1, p1, k1; repeat from * to last st, k1.
Repeat Rnds 1-4 for Wristers V Pattern.

SCARF
Using Long-Tail CO (see Special Techniques, page 158), CO 27 sts.
Begin 4x1 Rib; work even for 9 rows. Change to Scarf V Pattern; work
even until piece measures approximately 52", or to 2" less than desired
length from the beginning, ending with Row 8 of pattern. Work Rows
3–5 of V Pattern once. Change to 4x1 Rib; work even for 8 rows. BO all
sts in pattern.

WRISTERS (both alike)
CUFF
Using Long-Tail CO (see Special Techniques, page 158), CO 25 sts.
Divide sts among 3 needles [10-7-8]. Join for working in the rnd, being
careful not to twist sts; place marker (pm) for beginning of rnd. Begin
Wristers V Pattern; work even for 18 rnds.

HAND

Shape Thumb

NOTE: The purl sts on Needles 1 and 2 mark where you will work the increases on each Increase Rnd. You will work the increase on Needle 1 after the purl st, and the increase on Needle 2 before the purl st. If you prefer, you may omit placing the markers and use the purl sts as your markers.

Increase Rnd 1: *Needle 1:* K9, pm (optional), p1, LLI; *Needle 2:* RLI, pm (optional), p1, k6; *Needle 3:* Knit—27 sts [11-8-8]. Work even for 3 rnds.

Increase Rnd 2: Increase 2 sts this rnd, then every 4 rnds 3 times, as follows: *Needle 1:* Knit to marker (or to purl st if you didn't place a marker), slip marker (sm), p1, RLI, knit to end of needle; *Needle 2:* Knit to marker (or to purl st), LLI, sm, p1, knit to end of needle; *Needle 3:* Knit—35 sts [15-12-8]. Work even for 3 rnds.

Next Rnd: K10, place next 10 sts on holder for Thumb, removing markers if you placed them, knit to end—25 sts remain [10-7-8]. Work even for 3 rnds.

Next Rnd: Change to Wristers V Pattern, beginning with Rnd 2; work Rnds 2–4 three times (do not work Rnd 1). Knit 2 rnds. BO all sts very loosely knitwise.

THUMB

Transfer sts from waste yarn to 3 dpns, being careful not to twist sts. Rejoin yarn, using Backward Loop CO (see Special Techniques, page 158), CO 1 st—11 sts. Join for working in the rnd; pm for beginning of rnd.

Rnds 1–3: Knit.
Rnd 4: [K3, p1] twice, k3.
Rnd 5: K2, [p1, k1] 4 times, k1.
Rnds 6 and 7: Knit.
BO all sts very loosely knitwise.

FINISHING

Sew gaps at Thumb.

WE'RE STILL KNITTING

"I'M NOT THE SAME AUNT CHARLOTTE YOU REMEMBER," SHE tells me over the phone each time I call.

"And I'm not twelve anymore," I reply. We are both moving the way of all flesh. Aunt Charlotte is much closer to the finish line.

Married to my father's older brother, Morty Epstein, Aunt Charlotte taught in the New York City public schools for thirty-four years. When I was six and my brother Miles was born, she bought gifts for me, too: my first Dr. Seuss book, a large square of needlepoint canvas, and a ball of yellow wool. While other friends and relatives fussed over the new baby, Aunt Charlotte, always the teacher, listened to me read. And after that, she taught me how to stitch. Enchanted with my presents and my favorite aunt's attention, I couldn't bother being jealous of the new arrival.

In my footloose twenties, on my way to and from Israel, or Iowa, or upstate New York, I liked to pop in and visit with my aunt Charlotte and uncle Morty whenever I could. They lived close to JFK airport and were always ready to meet me there and bring me back to their house for a few days before I headed off on my next adventure. They were interested in whatever I did, whatever I was studying, and wherever I was going; their support helped give me roots and wings.

At some point during these short stays, probably after Aunt Charlotte retired from teaching, she and I would find ourselves alone.

Uncle Morty was finally getting to go to college. Their children, my cousins Michael and Janet, were busy raising their own children. With no one around to interrupt us, we discovered we both loved to knit, and that talking and knitting made an enjoyable afternoon.

My aunt is a dedicated pattern follower, and during those afternoons together she helped me understand why. She showed me that if you pay attention to what's written, your sweater can resemble the one the model wears.

Years passed, and with them came many life changes for me. I finished school, married, had three children, and settled down in the Midwest. When Aunt Charlotte and I had our knitting conversations, they were mainly on the phone, long distance.

When we did see each other, we grabbed our knitting time any way we could. One time, for example, was after her granddaughter's bat mitzvah, in the parking lot of a New Jersey synagogue with my kids arguing in the car and my husband discussing directions to the airport with my uncle.

That day, my aunt had a knitting question for me. There was a part of a baby sweater pattern she wasn't sure about; could I explain it? So we stood there companionably, discussing the proper way to count rows and the confusing nature of certain knitting terminology.

In 1999, at the age of eighty-three, Aunt Charlotte collapsed outside Columbia Presbyterian Hospital in New York City. On life support, she underwent open-heart surgery. Despite being given a three-percent chance of survival, she bounced back with her knitting needles, ready to make yet another baby sweater. This one would be for her newest great-grandchild.

My cousin Janet says her mother is like the Energizer Bunny. She just keeps going. Still, her near-death episode that year was a wake-up call for me, and I realized I needed to visit her. With three school-age kids, it wasn't easy getting away by myself. But we had to have some knitting time again.

Janet, a teacher like her mother, picked me up at the airport on a Friday after school. We drove straight to her parents' new home in a retirement community near Princeton, New Jersey. The four of us ate dinner at a local restaurant and caught up with all the news that gets left out of phone conversations. My uncle Morty and I talked politics a bit. Over coffee, back at their house, my cousin, my aunt, and I planned our Saturday. The centerpiece of the day was a trip to a yarn store. Another great-grandchild was expected, and this time Aunt Charlotte wanted to make a baby blanket. Janet, who had begun to knit, had a scarf in mind for one of her daughters. I had brought some socks to knit on, but I was game to check out the yarn and start something new.

After an early breakfast and coffee, we left Uncle Morty with the dishes and the *New York Times*. Our first stop was at a hospital supply store. Unsteady and unsure on her feet, Aunt Charlotte had been resisting using a walker. But today she was a gal on a yarn-shopping mission, and she needed wheels. She chose a spiffy red one.

"Looks like a Schwinn walker," Janet told her.

"Even has a basket in front for your knitting," I pointed out.

"Take her for a spin," said the salesman.

It was a warm, sunny October day. Aunt Charlotte moved into the walker. She took a few hesitant steps and then many confident ones. Radiantly, she strode along the sidewalk.

"Morty," she spoke into the cell phone my cousin held out for her. "I feel ten years younger!"

Newly mobile, Aunt Charlotte led the way to lunch. Then we were off to the yarn store. Again, she led the way. The only customers in the small shop, we were free to *ooh* and *aah* loudly, to break into our "outdoor" voices and bellow, "You have to see this!" or, "I found the perfect yarn for you!" We all found wool and patterns and more. We drove home anxious to start knitting.

After dinner, Uncle Morty went to bed early. With our needles clacking, my aunt, cousin, and I became a circle of chatter and laughter.

"Charlotte, aren't you coming to bed?" called Uncle Morty from their bedroom. It was close to one.

"No," said Aunt Charlotte. "I'm still knitting."

Years later, we are all still knitting, Aunt Charlotte, Cousin Janet, and me.

On the day before her ninety-fourth birthday, Aunt Charlotte doesn't need to remind me that she's not the same aunt I remember from my childhood. We are all forging into the uncharted territory of aging. We are all changing.

But some things do stay the same. Actually deepen. While working on a children's story about knitting, I found a historical note describing how loved ones, soon to be boarding ships, leaving hearth and home, possibly forever, held onto one end of a ball of yarn. The other end stayed with the aching hearts on shore. Unwinding as the boat sailed away, the ball ends were dropped when the yarn could no longer cover the distance. The wool was left floating on the water between them.

So it is with the mighty Mississippi River and the states that separate my aunt, my cousin, and me. But we hold fast to our wool, knitting our ends tightly, and never letting them go.

AUNT CHARLOTTE'S "YOU WON'T BELIEVE HOW EASY IT IS TO MAKE" JAM

It didn't take my cousin Janet long to respond to my recipe request. "Mom's jam," she told me. "You won't believe how easy it is to make." Easy and delicious on the toast of your choice.

This is a third-generation recipe. It was given to Aunt Charlotte by her mother, Minnie, who got it from a friend.

3 cups dried, loosely packed apricots, diced
4 cups crushed canned pineapple with juice
½ cup water
3 cups granulated sugar

In a large bowl, combine all the ingredients. Cover and let stand overnight at room temperature.

Transfer apricot mixture to a 4-quart saucepan, preferably one with a heavy bottom. Bring to a boil over medium heat, then lower heat and simmer, stirring gently, for about 30 minutes, until thick and soft (no liquid should remain). Remove from heat and cool. Spoon into glass jars. Store in refrigerator.

Makes approximately 6 cups.

NOTE: Simple recipes invite innovation, so I couldn't resist experimenting with this one. Substituting 1 cup diced candied ginger slices for 1 cup of the diced dried apricots and reducing the sugar to 2 cups resulted in a sweet, snappy spread. Janet suggests swirling some jam into whipped cream cheese, spreading on crackers, and seasoning with pepper.

SHOWN LEFT TO RIGHT: CELLULAR EYELET, EYELET CHECK, BUTTERFLY EYELET.

TRIO OF LACY WASHCLOTHS

DESIGNED BY THERESA GAFFEY

MANY YEARS AGO I GAVE MY AUNT CHARLOTTE A HANDknitted washcloth as a gift. She is still using it and often she tells me how much she loves it. I hope you will use this trio of patterns to create gifts for your favorite friends and family members.

. . . .

FINISHED MEASUREMENTS

10" x 10"

YARN

Lion Brand Recycled Cotton (72% recycled cotton / 24% acrylic / 2% other fiber; 185 yards / 100 grams): 1 skein #123 Sand makes 2 washcloths

NEEDLES

One pair straight needles size US 9 (5.5 mm); change needle size if necessary to obtain correct gauge.

GAUGE

16 sts and 27 rows = 4" (10 cm) in Eyelet Check; 17 sts and 28 rows = 4" (10 cm) in Cellular Eyelet; 16 sts and 26 rows = 4" (10 cm) in Butterfly Eyelet

STITCH PATTERN

EYELET CHECK
(multiple of 8 sts + 9; 12-row repeat)

Rows 1 and 5 (RS): K7, *p3, k5; repeat from * to last 2 sts, k2.

Rows 2 and 4: K2, *p5, k3; repeat from * to last 7 sts, p5, k2.

Row 3: K7, *p1, yo, p2tog, k5; repeat from * to last 2 sts, k2.

Row 6: K2, purl to last 2 sts, k2.

Rows 7 and 11: K3, *p3, k5; repeat from * to last 6 sts, p3, k3.

Rows 8 and 10: K2, p1, *k3, p5; repeat from * to last 6 sts, k3, p1, k2.

Row 9: K3, *p1, yo, p2tog, k5; repeat from * to last 6 sts, p1, yo, p2tog, k3.

Row 12: Repeat Row 6.

Repeat Rows 1–12 for Eyelet Check.

CELLULAR EYELET (multiple of 4 sts + 7; 8-row repeat)
Row 1 (RS): K2, p1, *k3, p1; repeat from * to last 4 sts, k4.
Row 2: K2, p2, *k1, p3; repeat from * to last 3 sts, k3.
Row 3: K2, p1, *k3, p1; repeat from * to last 4 sts, k4.
Row 4: K2, p2tog, *yo, k1, yo, p3tog; repeat from * to last 3 sts, yo, k3.
Row 5: K4, *p1, k3; repeat from * to last 3 sts, p1, k2.
Row 6: K3, *p3, k1; repeat from * to last 4 sts, p2, k2.
Row 7: K4, *p1, k3; repeat from * to last 3 sts, p1, k2.
Row 8: K3, yo, *p3tog, yo, k1, yo; repeat from * to last 4 sts, p2tog, k2.
Repeat Rows 1–8 for Cellular Eyelet.

BUTTERFLY EYELET (multiple of 10 + 4; 12-row repeat)
Rows 1 and 7 (RS): Knit.
Rows 2 and 8: K2, purl to last 2 sts, k2.
Rows 3 and 5: K2, *k2tog, yo, k1, yo, ssk, k5; repeat from * to last 2 sts, k2.
Rows 4 and 6: K2, p7, *slip 1 purlwise, p9; repeat from * to last 5 sts, slip 1 purlwise, p2, k2.
Rows 9 and 11: K7, *k2tog, yo, k1, yo, ssk, k5; repeat from * to last 7 sts, k2tog, yo, k1, yo, ssk, k2.
Rows 10 and 12: K2, p2, *slip 1 purlwise, p9; repeat from * to last 10 sts, slip 1 purlwise, p7, k2.
Repeat Rows 1–12 for Butterfly Eyelet.

WASHCLOTH

Eyelet Check Washcloth: CO 41 sts. Knit 2 rows. Begin Eyelet Check; work even until piece measures approximately 9¾" from the beginning, ending with Row 5 of pattern. Knit 2 rows. BO all sts knitwise.
Cellular Eyelet Washcloth: CO 43 sts. Knit 2 rows. Begin Cellular Eyelet; work even until piece measures 9¾" from the beginning, ending with Row 4 or 8 of pattern. Knit 3 rows. BO all sts knitwise.
Butterfly Eyelet Washcloth: CO 44 sts. Knit 2 rows. Begin Butterfly Eyelet; work even until piece measures approximately 9¾" from the beginning, ending with Row 7 of pattern. Knit 2 rows. BO all sts knitwise.

FINISHING

Block as desired.

LOOPS TO THE END

"Knitting is formed by a series of loops pulled through
loops to the end of time or to 'desired length.' ...
Be grateful for this and don't expect any more."
—Elizabeth Zimmermann, *Knitter's Almanac*

HAVE KNIT FOR BETTER AND FOR WORSE, IN SICKNESS AND IN health. I have knit while listening to the breathing of those just born and by the bedside of the dying. I have knit on bamboo, bone, wood, casein, plastic, aluminum, and several types of steel. Two needles. Four needles. Five needles. Circular needles. With wool, mohair, angora, cotton, bamboo, silk, acrylics, blends, and recently, cashmere.

I have knit fast. Slow. Mindlessly. Sometimes carelessly. I have let my stitches drop, my pattern wander. I have misread my gauge. And I have knit with care, intent, and concentration—complex lace and elaborate cables. I have knit mittens, hats, scarves, socks, shawls, washcloths, patches, and more—the utilitarian and the whimsical.

I have knit for the grateful and for the ungrateful. I have knit for friends, for family, for myself. And I have knit my bit for those in need. I have knit full of hope and in moments when hope has been harder to find.

I have knit and seen nothing. Not the dishes in the sink, the stars in the sky, or what's on TV. And I have knit and seen everything. The piles of laundry, the gentle fluttering of the first snow, and how the mystery ends.

THE OPINIONATED KNITTER

BY ELIZABETH ZIMMERMANN

*"Now, let us all take a deep breath, and forge on
into the future; knitting at the ready."*
—Elizabeth Zimmermann, *Woolgathering*, Spring 1969

Over the years, Elizabeth Zimmermann's books, all now knitting classics, have been a source of information, comfort, and inspiration to

Many, many times, I have knit, as my good friend Esther likes to say, my mouth shut. I have knit just to see the colors change. Just to feel the movement of my needles.

I have knit while walking, talking, reading, stopping at train crossings, waiting in checkout lanes, traveling on planes, and riding in cars.

I have knit by candlelight. By flashlight. During snowstorms. Tornados. Floods. I have knit thinking about the big questions. And I have knit thinking about what to make for dinner. I have knit while writing stories and while illustrating books—even this book. I have knit listening to my husband read articles of interest and concern. I have knit while he reads to himself. I have knit while we have discussed grave matters. Movie choices. Teen curfews.

I have knit to the hiss of espresso machines, amid those ordering half-caf cappuccinos, double shots, double foam. I have knit by my kitchen table, on my porch, in my bed, on the bench out at Fae Ridge Farm, and on the red couch at Home Ec Workshop. I have knit alone. I have knit sociably with those whose names I've never learned. And I

me. EZ, as she is known in the knitting universe, gave us timeless patterns, innovative techniques, and the courage to try them. She gave us descriptions, often very poetic, of a knitter's life. My favorite EZ book is *The Opinionated Knitter*, published in 2005, six years after her death. An endearing abundance of knitterly richness, it includes reproductions of her typed newsletters with many of her signature patterns, her own and others' advice on knitting them, full-color photos of her family modeling her creations, and highlights from her other books and journals. Also tucked into this bundling are some near-legendary recollections by family and friends of EZ, such as remembrances of her knitting on the backs of motorcycles and while engaged in a standoff in a one-way street. If you can own only one knitting book, let it be *The Opinionated Knitter*. Then, in pen, you can add your own words on the last pages of knitters' tributes to Elizabeth Zimmermann, the matriarch of American knitting.

have knit in the company of those whose names I'll never forget, those who are knit and purled forever into my heart. I have knit up conversations, correspondences with new knitters. Old knitters. Cranky knitters. Charitable knitters.

I have knit to replace the lost hat and to repair the worn-out heel. And I have knit to celebrate births, weddings, graduations, anniversaries—my anniversary. I have knit to celebrate kindness. And I have knit to express my regrets, my deepest sympathies, even when I know that what I knit is but a tiny gesture.

I have knit when nursing my babies and then while watching them sleep peacefully. I have knit at my children's fencing bouts, Tae Kwon Do tournaments, soccer games, tennis matches, swim meets, dance recitals, concerts, and teachers' conferences. Many, many times I have knit anxiously, worrying over them, my babies, young adults now, but forever my children.

Loops, wrote Elizabeth Zimmermann. Knitting is about loops. *Loops to the end of time*. Making them, I have knit myself a life.

GENIE'S HAT

I HAVE KNIT FOR HUSBANDS. AND I HAVE KNIT FOR THEIR WIVES. A few years ago I made a thick, ear-warming hat for Ed McCliment, a dear friend and neighbor. When I found out his wife, Genie, was borrowing his hat, I knew it was time to make Genie a hat of her own—with a little something extra. Something a bit dapper and fun—just like Genie.

. . . .

FINISHED MEASUREMENTS
Small (Medium, Large)
To fit Child (Adult Small/Medium, Adult Large)
NOTE: Child's size fits most children ages 4 and up. For a denser, super-warm Hat, work
the pattern (including the embellishments) 1 size larger
and felt it lightly in the washing machine, checking it every 2 or 3 minutes until the Hat is the size you want. Make sure not to leave it in too long, since there's no going back once it's felted.

FINISHED MEASUREMENTS
13¾ (14¾, 16)" circumference, unstretched

NOTE: Hat is meant to stretch to fit snugly. Work 1 size up for a looser fit.

YARN
Lion Brand Alpine Wool (77% wool / 15% acrylic / 8% rayon; 93 yards / 85 grams): 1 skein #224 Barley (MC)
Lion Brand Yarn Alpine Wool (100% wool; 93 yards / 85 grams): 1 skein each #123 Bay Leaf (A) and #115 Chili (B)
NOTE: Since the amount of B needed for the Berries is minimal, you may prefer to use yarn from your stash in a similar color.

One 16" (40 cm) long circular (circ) needle size US 10 (6 mm)
One set of five double-pointed needles (dpn) size US 10 (6 mm)
Change needle size if necessary to obtain correct gauge.

NOTIONS

Stitch marker; piece of cardboard cut to fit inside unstretched, finished
Hat; tapestry needle

GAUGE

14 sts and 20 rnds = 4" (10 cm) in Stockinette stitch (St st; knit
every rnd)

STITCH PATTERN

1x1 RIB
(multiple of 2 sts; 1-rnd repeat)
All Rnds: *K1, p1; repeat from * to end.

BRIM

Using circ needle and MC, CO 48 (52, 56) sts. Join for working in the
rnd, being careful not to twist sts; place marker (pm) for beginning of
rnd. Begin 1x1 Rib; work even for 4 (5, 6) rnds.

CROWN

Next Rnd: Change to St st (knit every rnd); work even until piece
measures 6 (6¼, 6½)" from the beginning. **NOTE:** You may determine
the required length here by measuring the hand of the intended wearer.
Traditionally, the distance from wrist to longest fingertip corresponds to
the distance from the bottom of the Hat to the point where the
decreases should begin. (I learned this neat trick from Stephanie
Pearl-McPhee's book *Knitting Rules!*)

SHAPE CROWN

NOTE: Change to dpns when necessary for number of sts on needles.
SIZES (MEDIUM, LARGE)
Next Rnd: *K(11, 5), k2tog; repeat from * to end—48 sts remain. Knit 1 rnd.

ALL SIZES

Next Rnd: *K6, k2tog; repeat from * to end—42 sts remain. Knit 1 rnd.
Next Rnd: *K5, k2tog; repeat from * to end—36 sts remain. Knit 1 rnd.
Continue as established, knitting 1 less st before each decrease, until 12 sts remain after finishing a knit rnd.
Next Rnd: *K2tog; repeat from * to end—6 sts remain.
Cut yarn, leaving a 5" tail. Thread tail through remaining sts, pull tight, and fasten off.

EMBELLISHMENTS

LONG STEM AND SMALL LEAF

Using dpns and A, CO 2 sts. Work I-Cord (see Special Techniques, page 158) 14 (15, 15)" long.
Row 1: Bring yarn to right-hand side of work, k1, yo, k1, turn—3 sts.
Row 2 and all WS Rows: Purl.
Row 3: K1, M1-r, k1, M1-l, k1—5 sts.
Row 5: Knit.
Row 7: Ssk, k1, k2tog—3 sts remain.
Row 9: Sk2p—1 st remains. Fasten off, leaving 12" tail.

SHORT STEM AND LARGE LEAF

Beginning 2" up from CO edge of Stem, pick up and knit 2 sts from side of Stem.
Row 1: Bring yarn to right-hand side of work, k1, yo, k1, turn—3 sts.
Row 2 and all WS Rows: Purl.
Row 3: K1, M1-r, k1, M1-l, k1—5 sts.
Row 5: K2, M1-r, k1, M1-l, k2—7 sts.
Row 7: Knit.
Row 9: K1, ssk, k1, k2tog, k1—5 sts remain.
Row 11: Ssk, k1, k2tog—3 sts remain.
Row 13: Sk2p— 1 st remains. Fasten off, leaving 12".

MEDIUM LEAF

Beginning where Short Stem branches from Long Stem, pick up and knit 1 st each from second and third sts of side of Short Stem I-Cord. Work 1 row of I-Cord.
Row 1: Bring yarn to right-hand side of work, k1, yo, k1, turn—3 sts.

Row 2 and all WS Rows: Purl.
Row 3: K1, M1-r, k1, M1-l, k1—5 sts.
Rows 5 and 7: Knit.
Row 9: Ssk, k1, k2tog—3 sts remain.
Row 11: Sk2p. Fasten off, leaving 12" tail.

FINISHING
Lightly steam block Stems and Leaves.

Place piece of cardboard inside Hat to help piece remain flat and prevent pins from catching both layers of Hat. Pin Long Stem to Hat (see photo), beginning at CO edge and working to Small Leaf, making sure not to twist Stem and Leaf. Pin Short Stem and Large and Medium Leaves in place. Remove cardboard.

Using A, sew Stems, sewing through center of I-Cord Stem sts, and making sure not to sew through both layers of Hat. Using tails, sew Leaves to Hat, sewing through center of edge st at each side of each Leaf.

BERRIES
Using tapestry needle and B, work 2 Berries as follows: Bring needle from WS to RS in desired location for first Berry (see photo). Holding needle close to Hat, wrap yarn 2–3 times around needle, then insert needle back into Hat just next to where you brought yarn up (but not in exact spot). Keep your thumb on wraps of yarn around needle, to hold them in position. Pull needle through until knot becomes secure. Repeat for second Berry.

ABBREVIATIONS

BO – Bind off.

Circ – Circular

CO – Cast on.

Dpn – Double-pointed needle(s)

K1-f/b – Knit into front and back loop of same stitch to increase 1 stitch.

K2tog – Knit 2 stitches together.

K – Knit.

LLI (left lifted increase) – Pick up stitch below last stitch on right-hand needle and place on left-hand needle; knit picked-up stitch through back loop.

M1-l (make 1-left slanting) – With tip of left-hand needle inserted from front to back, lift strand between 2 needles onto left-hand needle; knit strand through back loop to increase 1 stitch.

M1-p (make 1 purlwise-right slanting) – With tip of left-hand needle inserted from back to front, lift strand between 2 needles onto left-hand needle; purl strand through front loop to increase 1 stitch.

M1-r (make 1-right slanting) – With tip of left needle inserted back to front, lift strand between 2 needles onto left needle; knit strand through front loop to increase 1 stitch.

P2tog – Purl 2 stitches together.

Pm – Place marker.

P – Purl.

Rnd(s) – Round(s)

RLI (right lifted increase) – Pick up stitch below next stitch on left-hand needle and place it on left-hand needle; knit picked-up stitch.

RS – Right side

S2kp2 – Slip next 2 stitches together to right-hand needle as if to knit 2 together, k1, pass 2 slipped stitches over.

Skp (slip, knit, pass) – Slip next stitch knitwise to right-hand needle, k1, pass slipped stitch over knit stitch.

Sk2p (double decrease) – Slip next stitch knitwise to right-hand needle, k2tog, pass slipped stitch over stitch from k2tog.

Sm – Slip marker

Ssk (slip, slip, knit) – Slip next 2 stitches to right-hand needle one at a time as if to knit; return them to the left-hand needle one at a time in their new orientation; knit them together through back loops.

St(s) – Stitch(es)

Tbl – Through back loop

Tog – Together

WS – Wrong side

Wyib – With yarn in back

Yo – Yarn over (see Special Techniques, page 158)

SPECIAL TECHNIQUES

Backward Loop CO

Make a loop (using a slip knot) with working yarn and place it on right-hand needle (first st CO), *wind yarn around thumb clockwise, insert right-hand needle into front of loop on thumb, remove thumb and tighten st on needle; repeat from * for remaining sts to be CO, or for casting on at end of a row in progress.

Duplicate stitch

Thread tapestry needle with chosen yarn and leaving tail to be woven in later, *bring needle from WS to RS of work at base of st to be covered, pass needle under both loops (base of st above) above st to be covered; insert needle into same place where you started (base of st), and pull yarn through to WS of work. Be sure new st is same tension as rest of piece. Repeat from * for additional sts.

I-Cord

Using double-pointed needle, cast on or pick up required number of sts; working yarn will be at left-hand side of needle. *Transfer needle with sts to left hand, bring yarn around behind work to right-hand side; using a second double-pointed needle, knit sts from right to left, pulling yarn from left to right for first st; do not turn. Slide sts to opposite end of needle; repeat from * until I-Cord is length desired.

Long-Tail (Thumb) CO

Leaving tail with about 1" of yarn for each st to be cast-on, make a slip knot in yarn and place it on right-hand needle, with tail to front and working end to back. Insert thumb and fore-finger of left hand between strands of yarn so that working end is around forefinger and tail end is around thumb "slingshot" fashion; *insert tip of right-hand needle into front loop on thumb, hook strand of yarn coming from forefinger from back to front, and draw it through loop on thumb; remove thumb from loop and pull on working yarn to tighten new st on right-hand needle; return thumb and forefinger to original positions, and repeat from * for remaining sts to be CO.

Satin Stitch

Bring threaded needle from WS to RS of fabric at one edge of area to be covered. *At opposite edge of area, bring needle from RS to WS and back to RS, catching smallest possible bit of background fabric. Repeat from *, carefully tensioning stitches so work lies flat without puckering.

Yarn Over (yo) at Beginning of Row

If first st is to be knit, hold yarn to front (in front of needle with no sts), insert needle into first st to be worked, bring yarn over needle and knit; if first st is to be purled, bring yarn around needle from front to back, then to front (purl position) and purl. Be careful not to lose yo.

Yarn Over (yo) Other Than Beginning of Row

Bring yarn forward (to purl position), then place it in position to work next st. If next st is to be knit, bring yarn over needle and knit; if next st is to be purled, bring yarn over needle and then forward again to purl position and purl. Work yarn over in pattern on next row unless instructed otherwise.

ACKNOWLEDGMENTS

WITH MUCH GRATEFULNESS, I'D LIKE TO ACKNOWLEDGE THE KINDNESS, goodwill, generosity, and hard work of those who helped make this book possible.

Galleries of gratitude to the book's photographer, Jen Gotch, and her husband, Andrew, for his amazing yarn creations. For testing the patterns and knitting projects, I am indebted to an amazing crew of knitters: Robin Anderson (Victory Wristers), Peggy Fitzgerald (Playtime Cape), Lucy Freers and her mom, Jen Kaalberg Freers (Playtime Cape), Codi Josephson (Clutch of Inspiration), Kenda Stewart (Gussies). In addition, Suzanne Doerhsuk (Genie's Hat, Quick and Easy Socks) solved several nagging heel problems and sized the socks, as well as Quick and Easy Mittens and Genie's Hat. Jody Stouffer (Chicken Egg Warmers, Playtime Cape) helped me decipher my pattern notes. Alisa Weinstein (Zigzag Baby Blanket, Quick and Easy Mittens) came to my rescue more than once. Lisa Wilcox (Good Karma Slippers, Zigzag Baby Blanket) helped in so many ways, she deserves a Super Master Knitter pin. And quintuple thanks to designer Theresa Gaffey (Updated Ripple Afghan, Trio of Lacy Washcloths, Lacy Scarf) for writing five wonderful patterns.

For their culinary contributions, I'd like to thank Heidi Anderson, Janet Cohen, Charlotte Epstein, Genie McCliment, Esther Retish, Anne Ylvisaker, and Jon Zeltsman. When you try their creations, I think you'll be grateful, too.

For keeping knitting lights burning in Iowa City, I'd like to thank Edyie Stika and The Knitting Shoppe. For their assistance with content, direction, ideas, and inspiration, I humbly thank Natalie Blitt, Naomi Dagan Bloom, Babbie Cameron, Vanaja Chandran, Janet Cohen, Laura D'Alessandro, Janette Ryan-Busch, Suzanne Doershuk, Peggy Fitzgerald, Vicki Itzkowitz, Codi Josephson, Gerri Kantrowitz, Monica Leo, Ellen Mack, Rosalie Maggio, Irene Palnick, Anne Price, Joanne Seiff, Nan Trefz, Lisa Wilcox, People to People, Alisa Weinstein, Anne Ylvisaker, and Jon Zeltsman. Volumes of thanks to all of you.

For providing me with a quiet space to work uninterrupted, rooms of thanks to Julie Decker, Harvest Preserve Foundation, Inc., and Rosalie Maggio.

For their cheers and sympathetic understanding, an Almond Champagne thank you to the Tall Grass Writers: Carol Gorman, Jackie Briggs Martin, Claudia McGehee, and Anne Ylvisaker.

For her accurate tech editing, inches of gratefulness to Sue McCain. For carefully editing the final essays, a heartfelt thanks to Betty Christiansen. For her kind, steady, and sharp critical guidance, for teaching me to focus on one thing at a time, and, together with graphic designer Sarah Von Dreele at onethread, for guiding my illustrations into the adult world, I am infinitely grateful to my editor, Melanie Falick.

For all the opportunities and help they have given me, I am deeply grateful to the folks at the Lion Brand Yarn Company: David Blumenthal, Ilana Rabinowitz, Zontee Hou, and Amy Ross. In addition to providing a home for my writings, Lion Brand supplied all the yarn for the projects in this book. And for their interest and enthusiasm, a warm thank-you to all the readers of my Lion Brand essays.

For patiently enduring the two long years when my focus and attention were on this book, I lovingly thank my husband, Rody Gessner, and our daughters, Meera, Flory, and Lelia.

A final debt of gratitude is owed to all those who appear throughout the book. While taking some liberty with conversations quoted, I endeavored always to be true to the content. Memory is sometimes a faulty friend, and I offer my sincerest apologizes for any mistakes and my regrets to any names left out. From the heart and the heartland, a bushel and a peck of thanks to all.